An examination and confutation of a lawlesse pamphlet, intituled, A briefe answer to a late treatise of the Sabbath-day: digested dialogue-wise betweene two divines, A and B. By Dr. Fr. White, L. Bishop of Ely (1637)

Francis White

An examination and confutation of a lawlesse pamphlet, intituled, A briefe answer to a late treatise of the Sabbath-day: digested dialogue-wise betweene two divines, A and B. By Dr. Fr. White, L. Bishop of Ely
Brief answer to a late treatise of the Sabbath day
Treatise of the Sabbath-day.
White, Francis, 1564?-1638.
Printer's name from STC.
A confutation of STC 4137.7: Henry Burton. A brief answer to a late treatise of the Sabbath day (1635?); Burton's work answers STC 25385: Francis White. A treatise of the Sabbath-day (1635).
[8], 162 p.
London : Printed by R. B[adger] and are to be sold in S. Dunstans Churchyard in Fleetstreet, at the little shop turning up to Cliffords-Inne, 1637.
STC (2nd ed.) / 25379
English
Reproduction of the original in the Cambridge University Library

Early English Books Online (EEBO) Editions

Imagine holding history in your hands.

Now you can. Digitally preserved and previously accessible only through libraries as Early English Books Online, this rare material is now available in single print editions. Thousands of books written between 1475 and 1700 and ranging from religion to astronomy, medicine to music, can be delivered to your doorstep in individual volumes of high-quality historical reproductions.

We have been compiling these historic treasures for more than 70 years. Long before such a thing as "digital" even existed, ProQuest founder Eugene Power began the noble task of preserving the British Museum's collection on microfilm. He then sought out other rare and endangered titles, providing unparalleled access to these works and collaborating with the world's top academic institutions to make them widely available for the first time. This project furthers that original vision.

These texts have now made the full journey -- from their original printing-press versions available only in rare-book rooms to online library access to new single volumes made possible by the partnership between artifact preservation and modern printing technology. A portion of the proceeds from every book sold supports the libraries and institutions that made this collection possible, and that still work to preserve these invaluable treasures passed down through time.

This is history, traveling through time since the dawn of printing to your own personal library.

Initial Proquest EEBO Print Editions collections include:

Early Literature

This comprehensive collection begins with the famous Elizabethan Era that saw such literary giants as Chaucer, Shakespeare and Marlowe, as well as the introduction of the sonnet. Traveling through Jacobean and Restoration literature, the highlight of this series is the Pollard and Redgrave 1475-1640 selection of the rarest works from the English Renaissance.

Early Documents of World History

This collection combines early English perspectives on world history with documentation of Parliament records, royal decrees and military documents that reveal the delicate balance of Church and State in early English government. For social historians, almanacs and calendars offer insight into daily life of common citizens. This exhaustively complete series presents a thorough picture of history through the English Civil War.

Historical Almanacs

Historically, almanacs served a variety of purposes from the more practical, such as planting and harvesting crops and plotting nautical routes, to predicting the future through the movements of the stars. This collection provides a wide range of consecutive years of "almanacks" and calendars that depict a vast array of everyday life as it was several hundred years ago.

Early History of Astronomy & Space

Humankind has studied the skies for centuries, seeking to find our place in the universe. Some of the most important discoveries in the field of astronomy were made in these texts recorded by ancient stargazers, but almost as impactful were the perspectives of those who considered their discoveries to be heresy. Any independent astronomer will find this an invaluable collection of titles arguing the truth of the cosmic system.

Early History of Industry & Science

Acting as a kind of historical Wall Street, this collection of industry manuals and records explores the thriving industries of construction; textile, especially wool and linen; salt; livestock; and many more.

Early English Wit, Poetry & Satire

The power of literary device was never more in its prime than during this period of history, where a wide array of political and religious satire mocked the status quo and poetry called humankind to transcend the rigors of daily life through love, God or principle. This series comments on historical patterns of the human condition that are still visible today.

Early English Drama & Theatre

This collection needs no introduction, combining the works of some of the greatest canonical writers of all time, including many plays composed for royalty such as Queen Elizabeth I and King Edward VI. In addition, this series includes history and criticism of drama, as well as examinations of technique.

Early History of Travel & Geography

Offering a fascinating view into the perception of the world during the sixteenth and seventeenth centuries, this collection includes accounts of Columbus's discovery of the Americas and encompasses most of the Age of Discovery, during which Europeans and their descendants intensively explored and mapped the world. This series is a wealth of information from some the most groundbreaking explorers.

Early Fables & Fairy Tales

This series includes many translations, some illustrated, of some of the most well-known mythologies of today, including Aesop's Fables and English fairy tales, as well as many Greek, Latin and even Oriental parables and criticism and interpretation on the subject.

Early Documents of Language & Linguistics

The evolution of English and foreign languages is documented in these original texts studying and recording early philology from the study of a variety of languages including Greek, Latin and Chinese, as well as multilingual volumes, to current slang and obscure words. Translations from Latin, Hebrew and Aramaic, grammar treatises and even dictionaries and guides to translation make this collection rich in cultures from around the world.

Early History of the Law

With extensive collections of land tenure and business law "forms" in Great Britain, this is a comprehensive resource for all kinds of early English legal precedents from feudal to constitutional law, Jewish and Jesuit law, laws about public finance to food supply and forestry, and even "immoral conditions." An abundance of law dictionaries, philosophy and history and criticism completes this series.

Early History of Kings, Queens and Royalty

This collection includes debates on the divine right of kings, royal statutes and proclamations, and political ballads and songs as related to a number of English kings and queens, with notable concentrations on foreign rulers King Louis IX and King Louis XIV of France, and King Philip II of Spain. Writings on ancient rulers and royal tradition focus on Scottish and Roman kings, Cleopatra and the Biblical kings Nebuchadnezzar and Solomon.

Early History of Love, Marriage & Sex

Human relationships intrigued and baffled thinkers and writers well before the postmodern age of psychology and self-help. Now readers can access the insights and intricacies of Anglo-Saxon interactions in sex and love, marriage and politics, and the truth that lies somewhere in between action and thought.

Early History of Medicine, Health & Disease

This series includes fascinating studies on the human brain from as early as the 16th century, as well as early studies on the physiological effects of tobacco use. Anatomy texts, medical treatises and wound treatment are also discussed, revealing the exponential development of medical theory and practice over more than two hundred years.

Early History of Logic, Science and Math

The "hard sciences" developed exponentially during the 16th and 17th centuries, both relying upon centuries of tradition and adding to the foundation of modern application, as is evidenced by this extensive collection. This is a rich collection of practical mathematics as applied to business, carpentry and geography as well as explorations of mathematical instruments and arithmetic; logic and logicians such as Aristotle and Socrates; and a number of scientific disciplines from natural history to physics.

Early History of Military, War and Weaponry

Any professional or amateur student of war will thrill at the untold riches in this collection of war theory and practice in the early Western World. The Age of Discovery and Enlightenment was also a time of great political and religious unrest, revealed in accounts of conflicts such as the Wars of the Roses.

Early History of Food

This collection combines the commercial aspects of food handling, preservation and supply to the more specific aspects of canning and preserving, meat carving, brewing beer and even candy-making with fruits and flowers, with a large resource of cookery and recipe books. Not to be forgotten is a "the great eater of Kent," a study in food habits.

Early History of Religion

From the beginning of recorded history we have looked to the heavens for inspiration and guidance. In these early religious documents, sermons, and pamphlets, we see the spiritual impact on the lives of both royalty and the commoner. We also get insights into a clergy that was growing ever more powerful as a political force. This is one of the world's largest collections of religious works of this type, revealing much about our interpretation of the modern church and spirituality.

Early Social Customs

Social customs, human interaction and leisure are the driving force of any culture. These unique and quirky works give us a glimpse of interesting aspects of day-to-day life as it existed in an earlier time. With books on games, sports, traditions, festivals, and hobbies it is one of the most fascinating collections in the series.

The BiblioLife Network

This project was made possible in part by the BiblioLife Network (BLN), a project aimed at addressing some of the huge challenges facing book preservationists around the world. The BLN includes libraries, library networks, archives, subject matter experts, online communities and library service providers. We believe every book ever published should be available as a high-quality print reproduction; printed on-demand anywhere in the world. This insures the ongoing accessibility of the content and helps generate sustainable revenue for the libraries and organizations that work to preserve these important materials.

The following book is in the "public domain" and represents an authentic reproduction of the text as printed by the original publisher. While we have attempted to accurately maintain the integrity of the original work, there are sometimes problems with the original work or the micro-film from which the books were digitized. This can result in minor errors in reproduction. Possible imperfections include missing and blurred pages, poor pictures, markings and other reproduction issues beyond our control. Because this work is culturally important, we have made it available as part of our commitment to protecting, preserving, and promoting the world's literature.

GUIDE TO FOLD-OUTS MAPS and OVERSIZED IMAGES

The book you are reading was digitized from microfilm captured over the past thirty to forty years. Years after the creation of the original microfilm, the book was converted to digital files and made available in an online database.

In an online database, page images do not need to conform to the size restrictions found in a printed book. When converting these images back into a printed bound book, the page sizes are standardized in ways that maintain the detail of the original. For large images, such as fold-out maps, the original page image is split into two or more pages

Guidelines used to determine how to split the page image follows:

- Some images are split vertically; large images require vertical and horizontal splits.
- For horizontal splits, the content is split left to right.
- For vertical splits, the content is split from top to bottom.
- For both vertical and horizontal splits, the image is processed from top left to bottom right.

AN EXAMINATION AND CONFVTATION

of a Lawlesse Pamphlet,

INTITVLED,

A briefe Answer to a late Treatise of the SABBATH-DAY:

Digested Dialogue-wise betweene two Divines,
A and B.

By Dr. Fr. White, *L. Bishop of* Ely.

2 Cor. 13. *We can do nothing against the Truth, but for the Truth.*

Hieronymus, de Luciferianis, dicit : Facilius eos vinci posse, quam persuaderi.

LONDON,
Printed by R. B. and are to be sold in S. Dunstans Churchyard in Fleetstreet, at the little Shop turning up to Cliffords-Inne.
1637.

TO THE CHRISTIAN AND IVDICIOVS READER.

He *Reason and Occasion inducing my Superiours to imploy mee in a service of the Church, for penning and publishing a Treatise of the Sabbath, and of the Lord's-day, is delivered* in my Epistle Dedicatory to the Lord's Grace of Canterbury: *And my intention in performing thereof, was to deliver and maintaine the Orthodoxall Doctrine of the Primitive Church, and the Doctrine of the Church of England,* authorised by the Lawes and Statutes of our Kingdome, *against the Sabbatarian Error of one* Theophilus Brabourne: *and because this Errant had grounded the most of his Arguments, upon certaine Principles borrowed from some* Moderne Teachers *of our owne Nation, I was compelled to examine and confute the same.*

This *service being with much Care and Diligence performed*

by

To the READER.

by me, I expected some thankes for convicting and converting that Errant, and for preventing the farther spreading, and infection of his Error: But *at least I presumed to have obtained a charitable Construction of such Passages in my Treatise, as were subservient to a farther discovery of Verity: and that if any had found cause of dissenting from me, they would in a charitable and peaceable manner, have propounded their Exceptions.*

It hath *now so fallen out, that contrary both to my desert and expectation,* A certaine clamorous and audacious Scripturient, *a Person of a very weak judgement, but yet exceeding confident, and arrogant, hath vented a* Lawlesse, *and unlicensed* Pamphlet, *digested* Dialogue-wise &c, *wherein he Proclaimeth with open mouth, that my Treatise of the Sabbath* overthroweth the publike Doctrine of the Church of England, touching that Question.

Now, *the whole matter and frame of his Dialogue is so rude, and indigested,* and the Author thereof is so notorious for his ignorance, envy, and presumption, *that it rather merits execration, than confutation:* and many Persons of worth and quality, *have perswaded me rather to contemne, than to confute, either* the worke, or the workeman.

But *when I consider the cause it selfe, and the humour of factious people, who are alwaies ready to conceive their owne fancies, to be irrefragable* Verities, *if they passe in publike without just reproofe; I conceive, it can be no indiscretion in Me, or dishonour for Me, to appeare in defence of Veritie,* against falsitie and iniquitie, *how base and unworthy soever the Author is, with whom I shall contest.*

Now all which *I shall desire of the judicious Reader is;* first, *that he take into consideration, the maine accusation of the Dialogist, which is;* That in my Treatise of the Sabbath, I have overthrowne the publike Doctrine of the CHURCH of ENGLAND touching this Question.

Secondly,

To the READER.

Secondly, *that he will duely and impartially consider, and examine in the ballance of* true judgement, *the Adversaries Exceptions, and Objections against my Arguments and Positions; and my Answere, and confutation of the same.*

Concerning *the maine accusation of the Objector before mentioned, the Reader may easily discerne the falsity and iniquitie of it : for the Doctrine of the Church of England concerning the Sunday, and other Holy dayes, is in plaine and expresse termes delivered in the Statute of* Quinto *and* Sexto *of* King EDWARD *the sixt, cap. 3. in manner following*:

Neither *is it to be thought, that there is any certaine time, or number of dayes* prescribed in holy Scripture, *but that the appointment both of the time, and also of the number of the dayes is left* by the authoritie of God's Word, *to the libertie of* CHRIST's *Church to be determined, and assigned orderly in every Countrey*, by the discretion of the Rulers and Ministers thereof, as they shal judge most expedient to the setting forth of God's glorie, and the edification of their people. *Be it therefore enacted, by the King our Sovereigne Lord, with the assent of the Lords Spirituall and Temporall, and the Commons in this present Parliament assembled, & by the authority of the same, that all the dayes hereafter mentioned, shall bee kept and commanded to be kept holy dayes, and none other : that is to say* : All Sundayes in the yeere ; *The dayes of the Feasts of the Circumcision of our Lord* JESUS CHRIST ; *of the Epiphanie; of the Purification of the blessed* Virgine ; *of S.* Matthias *the Apostle, &c. And that none other day shall be kept holy day, or to abstaine from lawfull bodily labour.*

The *former Statute being repealed*, Anno primo Mariæ, cap. 2. *was revived*, An. prim. R. JACOBI, cap. 25. *and is at this day in force, as appeareth by the booke of Statutes*; pag. 894. *and by the judgement of the* Reverend Iudges, *and* Masters in our Lawes.

A Second passage, *which I desire the judicious Reader to*

observe

To the READER.

observe, is; That the Doctrine concerning the Sabbath day, and the Lord's day, maintained in my Treatise, agreeth exactly with the unanimous Tenet of the Orthodoxall Catholike Church of ancient times: and the same agreeth likewise with the Tenet, both of all the Schoole Doctours, ancient and moderne, and also with the Tenet of the best learned and most religious Divines of the reformed Churches *beyond Sea:* And lastly, the same is agreeable to the Tenet of the Holy Martyrs of our owne Church; Bishop Cranmer, Iohn Frith, William Tindall, D. Barnes &c. And the other opinion; That the fourth Commandement is a Precept of the Law of Nature, and purely and intirely Morall: And that the observation of the Lord's Day is expresly commanded by that Precept of the Decalogue, is a novell Position, repugnant to all, or most Orthodoxall Divines, who have instructed Christian people in the wayes of godlinesse, in former or moderne times.

Every one of the former passages, is so fully prooved and confirmed in my Treatise of the Sabbath, that no just exception can be taken against my proceeding, in handling this Question: and therefore the boldnesse, and impudency of this blattering Dialogist is detestable, when he affirmeth, that my Treatise of the Sabbath overthroweth the Doctrine of the Church of England.

Lastly, all the Reward which I desire to reape for my travell in this, or in any other service of the Church, is, that the Truth which I have faithfully delivered, may bee maintained, and my integrity be protected, against gracelesse, impudent, and irreverent Calumniators, such as the Author of the Dialogue hath proclaimed himselfe to be, in this, and in some other of his lewd and lawlesse Pamphlets.

For although this Dialogue penner hath concealed his name, yet *Ex ungue Leonem,* the world may easily conjecture who the Creature is, by his foule paw: The Scope of his writing in his Pamphlets, is, to magnifie his owne zeale, piety, and integrity,

To the READER.

to perswade the World, that he alone is left a Prophet of the LORD, and is guided with the spirit of Verity and Fidelity; and that the present Fathers and Rulers of our CHURCH, and other conformable Persons who comply with them, are little better than Hirelings and blinde Guides: And (besides his ignorance, which is notorious) the violent Man, is so far transported with bitter Zeale, that whatsoever proceeds from him, is litigious, clamorous, scandalous, and abusive: and his Pamphlets are fraughted with such Materials, as are apt to poyson Christian people with contempt and hatred of Ecclesiasticall Government, and present Religion established in our CHURCH. Also he is possessed with a gracelesse and malignant humour, to wit, looke whatsoever gives all other judicious and godly Persons best content, enrageth him against such as are imployed in the Governement and publike service of the CHURCH.

But I shall detaine my Reader no longer from the Examination of this Man's Quarrels and Objections vented in his Dialogue; and my Answer, and Reply shall make it evident, that the Doctrine propounded, and maintained in my Treatise of the Sabbath (maugre the malice of this Blatterant) standeth firme, and is not subject to any just Reproofe.

Πάντα δοκιμάζετε, καὶ τὸ καλὸν κατέχετε. Prove all things, and hold fast that which is good.

A devout Friend of all those, who are lovers of Truth and Peace.

Fra. Eliens.

The Title and Inscription of the Dialogue.

A
BRIEFE ANSWER,
TO A LATE TREATISE
OF THE *SABBATH-DAY*:
Digested *Dialogue-wise*, betweene
two Divines, *A* and *B* : beginning
with these words,

Brother, *You are happily met.*

HE saying of Saint *Augustine* may justly bee applied to this Dialogist, to wit: *It is an easie matter, for such as cannot be silent, to frame babling answers: and none are so forward to crake, as empty Casks puffed up with Vanity*; but although *Vanity can make lowder noise than Verity, yet it will have no power to prevaile against Verity.* [a]

a Aug. *de Civ. Dei.* l.5.c.27. Facile est cuiquam videri respondisse, qui tacere noluerit. Aut quid est loquacius vanitate? Quæ non ideo potest quod veritas, quia si voluerit, etiam plus potest clamare quàm veritas.

B   Now

(2)

Now upon due examination *of* the Cavils and Objections contained in this Dialogue; it will be manifest, that the Author thereof is not a person in any measure qualified with endowments and abilities, requisite and necessary for such an Undertaker: *to wit, with sound Iudgement, sufficient Learning, love of Verity,* together with *Modesty and Humility*: *For* instead of solid and substantiall proceeding, *the* judicious Reader shall finde nothing in his Dialogue, *but presumptuous Dictats; absurd* and *non-concluding Objections; perversion* of the true state of the question; *solution* of Arguments, by denying the Conclusion, and pretermission of the Premises; *abuse* of Terms when he citeth Authors; *rude* and irreverent Behaviour [b], toward the Person & Calling of Him, whom he stileth his Adversary. *And* the most of his Positions concerning the Sabbath, and the Lord's-day, are repugnant to the common sentence of all learned and godly Divines, who have treated of this Argument in ancient or moderne Times.

b *Hieron. ad Nepotian.* Nolo te declamatore esse, & tabulen, garrulum parenetione, sed mysteriorum peritum, & Sacramentorum Dei tui eruditissimum. *Verba volvere, & celeritate dicendi apud imperitum vulgus admirationem sui facere, indoctorum hominum est. Attrita frons interpretatur sæpe quod nescit, & cum aliis persuaserit, sibi quoque usurpat scientiam.*

This rude and gracelesse creature had not the honesty to consider, that the Author of that Treatise, against which he barketh, *undertook* his Work by command of High and lawfull Authority: *and* the true Reason, inducing his *Superiours* to imploy him in this service, was urgent and important.

For

For a pestilent, and subtile Treatise was published (and dedicated to his Royall Majestie,) *in which the Author maintained, with much confidence,* [a] *and with sundry probable Arguments; That the old Sabbath of the 4th Commandement (and not the Sunday or Lord's-day of every weeke) ought by divine Law to be religiously observed in the Christian Church.*

Now the Grounds and Principles, upon which that *Sabbatarian* builded his errour, *were* the same Positions and Dictats, which this *Dialogue-weaver,* and some late Teachers of our owne Nation, have peremptorily maintained, in their Pamphlets, Lectures, and Catechismes: *and* had these Positions, and Dictats beene divine Verities, it would have beene impossible to have solved *Th. Brab.* his Objections in a cleere and substantiall manner.

For it is most certaine, that *the Sabbath-day commanded to be kept holy in the 4th Precept of the Decalogue, was Saturday, the seventh and last day of the Weeke* [b]: *That* day of the weeke, in which Almighty God ceased, or rested, from the worke of prime Creation: *That* very day, which the *Iewes* perpetually observed in their Generations: The same day, concerning which the Pharisees so often contested with our Saviour: *The day* wch was a figure of Christ his resting in his grave: *and* of our Christian Sabbatisme, or spirituall Resting from sin. *Reade* the Bishops Treatise, *pag.* 182, 183.

[a] Theoph. Brab. *I am tyed in conscience, rather to depart with my life, than with the truth: so captivated is my conscience, and enthralled to the Law of God.* H. B. Law and Gosp. reconcil. 1 p. Dedicat. *A Booke lately come forth, which would utterly evacuate the Lord's-day, and reduce us to the Iewish Sabbath againe, which will be a worke so much the more necessary, by how much this Iewish Sabbatarian findes already, many idle & giddybrained Christians to imbrace this his Booke, which is written, with a mighty, confident, and Gyant like spirit, as if the arguments thereof were invincible.*

[b] Aug. Ep. 119. c.10. Sabbatum obseruandum est pro populo in octo corporali tempore diei, & ad designandum

set sanctificationis in requiem Spiritus Sancti: Nam in eorum legibus antiquis *moris*
per omnes priores dies, de solo Sabbato dictum est, et sanctificavit Deus diem septimam.

Now this being a certaine and undeniable verity, *it will* be consequent, *that* if the 4th Commandement of the Decalogue be *simply, entirely, and properly morall, and of the Law of Nature* (as this Objecter pretendeth :) *Then* the Saturday-Sabbath of every Weeke must be observed by Christians, and not the Sunday or Lord's Day in the place thereof.

A necessity therefore was cast upon *the Bishop* to examine this, and such like *Sabbatarian Principles*, and to demonstrate the falsity of them: For He was not otherwise able, by any course of true Disputation, to solve *Th. Brab.* his objections. *Sine causa enim aliquis ramos conatur incidere, si radicem non conatur evellere:* [a] It will prove lost labour, for any one to endeavour to lop off the boughes or branches of a Tree, if he shall still suffer the Roote to grow.

[a] Aug. li. 50. Homil. 8.

Also because *Th. Brab.* had, upon the former Principles, stiled the Lord's Day *an Idoll, and a Superstitious Tradition: The Bishop* thought it his duty to vindicate the honour of that Day; and to deliver the true grounds, upon which the Christian Church observeth it: *also* to declare the Antiquity of the Observation thereof: *and* the more to advance the honour of the Day, he collected out of the Primitive Fathers, Ecclesiasticall Histories, and Ancient Records, sundry remarkeable observations, concerning the Religious use, and sanctification of this Day, *Pag* 196. &c.

Lastly, because some Novell Teachers, here in England, had wronged this Day, by converting it into a Legall Sabbath; and likewise they had presumed, without any lawfull authority, to lay heavy and unreasonable burdens upon God's people: *Affirming that all bodily exercise, and all civill passe-time and Recreation, (although the same be sober and honest) is simply unlawfull, upon all houres of the Lord's Day; and* not only unlawfull, *but a mortall and enormious crime,* of the same quality, and in quity, with *Murder, Adulterie, Theft,* &c. The *Bishop* had just reason, to discover the error and falsitie of such principles and arguments, upon which these presumptuous Dogmatizers grounded their rigid edicts, *pag.* 235. unto *pag.* 250.

Now after all this the *Bishop* himselfe is perswaded, and so likewise are his *Honourable and Religious Superiours, that* he hath performed faithfull, profitable, and necessary service to the Church (whereof he is a member) in composing and publishing his Treatise of the Sabbath: *And* likewise his confidence is, *that* those *honourable and Reverend Commanders,* who imployed him in this religious service, will ever protect him, [a] against base, envious, and scurrilous abuses and detractions (such as hee is rudely, and injustly loaded withall) by *this unmannerly, and foule-mouth'd Dialogue-Broacher.*

Neverthelesse, if any learned, judicious, and modest Reader *shall* at any time note, or observe any passages in his Treatise, seeming to them repugnant to Orthodoxall Verity, [b] *let* them proceed soberly, substantially, and modestly, in propounding their exceptions; [c] *The Bishop* is, and ever

[a] *Aug. de Doctr. Christ.* Sic Doctor bonam eligat vitam, ik etiam bonam non negligat famam.

[b] *Aug. de Trin. li.* 3. In omnibus literis meis non solum pium lectorem, sed etiam liberum correctorem desidero.

[c] *Ib.* Noli meis literas ex tui opinione vel contentione, sed ex divina lectione, vel incomussa ratione corrigere.

ever will bee ready (without giving the least offence) to yeeld them a just and reasonable satisfaction.

But *rude, envious, and clamorous Carpers* (such as this Dialogue-Broacher is, and hath ever bin [c]) are incompetent Iudges, in Questions and Controversies of this quality: *for* such Mens Tractats, and Pamphlets, containe nothing, but only that, which is Verball, Illiterate, and no wayes sufficient to discover or settle Truth. *The end also of their writing is not Verity: but* they study onely to flatter *an irregular Multitude*, which is adverse to Ecclesiasticall Regiment setled in our Church: *and* the *Leaders of this Anarchicall Sect*, by applying themselves to the humour of *these Proselytes*, gaine popular applause, [d] and likewise authority to make their own fancies, and traditions to be no lesse esteemed, than Divine Oracles.

For being wily as Serpents, they have by long and subtill experience observed, *that* impetuou speaking, clamorous inveighing, virulent declaming prevaile more with that generation, tha solid, materiall, and substantiall disputing. [e] *No* this verball forme hath the *worthlesse penner* o this Dialogue observed, both in this, and in all other his *unlicensed Pamphlets*.

[c] Hieron *ed'uian. Gloriæ animal, & popularis auræ venatio incipiunt.*

[d] Greg. Nazian. orat. 8. de pace. Ex rebus novis, charitatem sibi venantur. Chrys. In Iob. Ho. 65. Prava doctrina nihil aliud est, quam inanis gloriæ filia.

[e] Hieron ad. Nepotian. Nihil tam facile, quam vilem plebeculam, & indoctam concionem linguæ volubilitate decipere, quæ, quicquid non intelligit, plus miratur. Id e. Ruffin. li. 1. Quotidie in plateis totus humeris stultorum nares verberat, & obtorto scorpione dentes mordenti sua quære; & miramur, si imperitorum libri lectorem inveniant?

Th

The Bishop of Ely his Positions, concerning the Old Sabbath Day, and the Lord's-Day, which are opposed by the Dialogue-Broacher.

Thesis 1. The Law of the fourth Commandement, concerning the religious observation of the Seventh Day Sabbath of every weeke, was not *purely morall, or of the Law of Nature, like* as were the other nine Commandements of the Decalogue.

This Position is confirmed by Demonstrative arguments, in the *Bishops* Treatise of the Sabbath, *pag.* 26. unto *pag.* 37.

Thesis 2. The Law of the fourth Commandement, concerning the Seventh Day Sabbath, was Legall, in respect of the speciall Day designed by the letter of that Commandement. *The same Law, in respect of the literall Object thereof, is ceased under the Gospell, and obligeth not Christians to the religious observation thereof, as it did the Iewes in time of the Old Law.*

This Position is confirmed by many weighty arguments, and by the Vnanimous testimony of the Ancient Fathers. *Page* 6. 7. 8. 148. 161. 276.

Thesis 3. The Christian Church, in the New Testament, hath received *no speciall, or expresse divine precept,* in holy Scripture commanding the same,

same, to observe any one particular, or individuall day of every weeke, rather than another, for their Sabbath: *Neither* hath the Christian Church received any Divine mandate, to observe any day of the weeke, according to the rule of the fourth Commandement, *pag.* 189. 239.

Thesis 4ᵃ. The observation of the Lord's-day, is not grounded upon the particular Law of the fourth Commandement; But onely *upon the Equity of that Commandement, and* upon the practice and example of the *holy Apostles,* and of the Primitive Church. *And* after such time as the Persecutions of the Christian Church by Infidels ceased; *Then* godly Lawes and *Canons* were framed by *Constantine* the great, and by other succeeding Emperors, *Theodosius, Valentinian, Archadius, Leo,* and *Antoninus,* and by *Bishops* in their Synods, for the religious observance of the Lord's-day, *pag.* 109, 110. 135. 143. 189. 211.

Thesis 5ᵃ. The Sabbath day of the fourth Commandement, and the Lord's-day, both in holy Scripture, and in the writings of the godly Fathers, are made two distinct dayes of the weeke: *Neither* was it the ordinary stile of the Fathers, and Primitive Church, to name the Lord's-day *the Sabbath-day, in a proper and literall sense,* to wit, in such a sense as the *Iewes* stiled their Seventh day the Sabbath day, *pag* 201, 202.

Thesis 6ᵃ. There is no Divine Law extant in the old, or in the New Testament, prohibiting all secular labour, and all bodily exercise, and honest recreation, upon some part of the Lord's-day, namely

namely at such time of the day, as the religious offices thereof are ended: *much lesse* is there found any divine Law, which maketh honest and sober recreation, in manner aforesaid, an enormous crime, equall to Murder, and to Adultery, *pag.* 229. unto *pag.* 267.

Thesis 7. The Sanctification of one particular day in seven, is neither any principle of the Law of nature, nor yet an immediate Conclusion of the same, neither is the same commanded by any written Evangelicall divine Law: neverthelesse the same is consonant to the *Equity of the* 4th *Commandement of the Decalogue*; and besides, The religious observation of one day in seven, is a convenient time, for GOD's publique and solemne worship; and *the Christian Church in al ages, since the Apostles*, hath deputed one weekely Seventh-day, to the fore-said end: And therefore it is a thing just and reasonable, to continue the same observation, *pag.* 91.

Thesis 8. There is no expresse Commandement written in the New Testament, concerning the religious observation of the Sunday of every weeke, rather than of any other convenient day or time. Neverthelesse, because the Christian Church *ever since the Apostles age*, hath beene accustomed to observe this weekely-day; and it is a received Tradition, that the holy Apostles themselves were the authors of this observation: and also the maine reason upon which this observation was first grounded (to wit, *the Resurrection of* CHRIST, upon the day, called the LORD's-day,) is a just and weighty motive to induce Christian

C

ſtian people, to obſerve this day in the honour of CHRIST, and to teſtifie their rejoycing and thankefulneſſe, for the benefit of our SAVIOUR's Reſurrection: Therefore *it is not expedient, decent, or agreeable to equity and good reaſon, to alter the long continued obſervation* of this day, into any other new day or time, *pag.* 152.

Incipi

Incipit PROLOGUS.

A. Brother you are happily met.
B. And you Brother also.
A. I would I might spend an houre or two with you in private conference, in a point wherein I have of late been not a little perplexed.
B. Why, what is the matter Brother?
A. Have you not seene a late Treatise of the Sabbath-day, published by an *eminent Antistes* in this Church?
B. Yes, I have both seene and perused it.
A. I pray you, what thinke you of it?
B. I thinke it is *a very dangerous Booke*.
A. What meane you by that?
B. I mean *dangerous to the Authour*, if it were well examined, before *competent judges*.
A. How so, I pray you?
B. Because it overthrowes the Doctrine of the Church of England, in the point of the Sabbath.

A. Pardon me, that seemes to mee impossible.

B. Why?

A. Because he saith expresly in the very title page of his booke: That it containeth a defence of the Orthodoxall Doctrine of the Church of England, against Sabbatarian Novelty. And therefore I am confident, he will looke to make that good.

B. Be not too confident, you know the Proverb, *Fronti rara fides*: The foulest causes may have the fairest pretences.

Answ. The substance of the precedent interlocutory babble is: *The Bishops Booke is a dangerous booke, and that to himselfe, if it were examined before Competent judges: for* contrary to the title of the booke, *it overthrowes the Doctrine of the Church of England, in the point of the Sabbath.*

Our answer to this accusation is, 1. that if we will rightly understand the quality of it, we must first of all define who are *Competent judges*. *Now* the holy Scripture, The Law of reason, and all prudent men require these properties following, to the Constitution of *Competent judges*: 1. *Lawfull authority*: 2. *Sufficient learning* and knowledge: 3. *Feare of God*: 4. *Wisedome*: 5. *Integrity* and love of Verity.

2. *The Bishops* Treatise of the Sabbath *hath* already

ready beene examined by judges qualified in manner aforesaid: *Namely*, by the *two most Reverend Arch-Bishops*: *by* many *Reverend Bishops*: *by* the *Honourable Court of High Commission*: *by* many Reverend and learned *Deanes*: *by* many *Doctors*, and *Professors of Theologie*: *by* some of the learned *Readers in Divinity*, of both Vniversities: *by Noble and Prudent Statesmen*: *by* eminent *Professors of both Laws*, civill, and temporall: *and* the *Kings Majesty himselfe, the Bishops Soveraigne Lord and Master*, hath graciously accepted it: *and* if these before named, shall not be esteemed competent judges; *Our* desire is to be enformed by our *Brother. B. who*, in our Church or Kingdome, are competent judges? *but* especially let him resolve us, *who* shall be those competent Iudges, to whose sentence hee will submit the examination of his owne unlicensed pamphlets.

3 *The Bishop* hath not onely affirmed in the title page of his Treatise, that *it* containeth a Defence of the Orthodoxall Doctrine of the Church of England, &c. *but* he likewise hath confirmed the same by arguments and testimonies irrefragable. *Therefore Brother. B.* his proverbiall sentence, *Fronti rara fides*, is not χτὶ παντὸς, *for* it admitteth an exception, to wit, *credit* ought at all times to bee given to the *Frontispice* of every booke, which confirmeth that which is contained in the same by weightie and effectuall arguments.

Now the conclusion from the Premises is: *The Bishops Booke can prove no dangerous Book, either to himselfe, or to any other, if it were duely examined, by lawfull and competent Iudges.*

C 3   A

(14)

A. That is true you say. *But* yet I canno[t] be perſwaded, that ſo great a Perſonag[e] would ſo farre overſhoot, as to give tha[t] advantage to thoſe, whom he makes his adverſaries. *Nay*, you know his Booke i[s] dedicated to the *Arch-Biſhop of Canterbury* by whoſe direction, and that according t[o] his *ſacred Majeſty* his command, he was ſe[t] upon this work : *both* for the preventing o[f] miſchiefe, (as himſelfe ſaith in his Epiſtl[e] Dedicatory to the ſaid *Arch-Biſhop.*) and t[o] ſettle the Kings good Subjects, who have long time beene diſtracted about Sabbatarian queſtions. *Now* if he maintaine not, but (as you ſay) overthrow the Doctrine of the Church of England, he will have ſmall thankes from *his ſacred Majeſty* for his paines, *who* is the Defender of the Faith of the Church of England, *and* hath often ſolemnly proteſted, and that in his publike Declarations in print, *that* he will never ſuffer therein the leaſt innovation. And what thankes then can hee expect from the
Arch-Biſhop,

Declaration about the Diſſolving of the Parliament. And Declaration before the 39. Articles.

BP. trow you? *And* instead of preventing, he will pull on greater mischiefs; *And* in stead of setling the Kings good Subjects, he will fill their minds with greater distractions. *And* therfore Brother, in so saying you lay a heavy charge upon him. *It* is dangerous so to charge a Person of that Dignity, and Esteeme in the world. *Take heede* therefore **what you say.** *You* know also, that he is a great Scholer, deeply learned, a Reverend Father of the Church, so as *his judgment is taken almost for an Oracle.*

Answ. The summe of the former discourse is: *That* the Bishop can expect small thankes from the *Arch-Bishop of Canterbury*, to whom his Booke is dedicated: *or* from his *Majesty*, who will suffer no innovation in Religion: *if* he being of note for learning, and a Bishop of the Church, *hath*, in stead of setling the mindes of the Kings loving Subjects, distracted, or led them into error.

To this Verball discourse *it* is answered, that the Bishop hath already received approbation of his worke from his *sacred Majesty*: *and* as much thankes, and respect from the *Lord's Grace of Canterbury*, as a faithfull person can expect, or desire from a *Superior*: *and* continuing as he hath begun, he is in no danger to lose either *his Majesties*, or the *Arch-Bishops*, or any other worthy Persons lawfull favour.

a The

2 The Author (with thankfulnesse to God) protesteth, that He having bestowed above two hundred of his bookes, upon Persons (among which, many were) of great worth and quality, hath never as yet received so much as one check or affront from any one, since a three fold impression of the Book: *And* the Dialogue-deviser is the first *Satan* (so far as the Bishop is hitherto informed) *who hath fomed out his gall and venom against it*: *Sed quamvis libraverit accusationis suæ hastas, & totis adversus nos viribus interserit: credimus in Deo salvatore, quod scuto circumdabit veritas ejus, & cum Psalmista cantare poterimus: Sagittæ parvulorum factæ sunt sagittæ eorum;* although he hath with all his might bent his Speare, and darted his Weapons against us, yet wee trust in *God* our *Saviour*, that the shield of verity shall protect us, so that we may say with the Psalmist Their arrowes shall be as the arrowes of children. *Hier. adv. Ruffin. lib.* 1.

3 The Treatise is so farre from distracting the Kings loving Subjects, which are of a loyall and peaceable disposition; that many intelligent persons, who have diligently read, and examin'd the same (having in former time been doubtfull,) are now setled in a firme resolution, never to bee distracted with *Sabbatarian fancies* any more.

A. You know what is said in a late *book* allowed by Authority: *That the holy Fathers in God, the Bishops, are to be guides in Divinity, to the whole Clergie of inferiour Order; So as all Priests are to submit to their godly judgements in all matters appertaining to Religion.* And the reason is given; because the Fathers of the Church now and alwayes do, in the great mystery of godlinesse, comprehend many things which the common people doe not: *Yea, also some things which Ministers of the inferiour Order doe not apprehend. So as it is expected of those Holy Prelates, that we must lay our hand on our mouth when they speake, and be altogether regulated by their profound dictats.*

B. I remember well the Booke, *and* I cannot but wonder, that those passages were not expunged, with many others, when the Book was called in, and then the second time published *You know we live in a learned age* [a], *and we deny the Popes infallibility*,

Communion Booke Cases expounded by Reve.

[a] *One, of which ...*

infalibility, or that it can convey it selfe, as from the head, *and so confine it selfe within the reines of the body of the Prelacy*: Or that a Rotchet can confer this grace *Ex opere operato*. *And beleeve me Brother, when we see such a Papall spirit begin to perk up in this our Church, is it not high time, trow you, to look about us? Shall we stumble at the Noone-day, and in the Meridian of the Gospell close our eyes, and become the sworne Vassals of blinde Obedience* [b]? No, no: *In this case therefore, were Goliah himselfe the Champion, I would by Gods grace try a fall with him.*

Answ. It *bold Bayard* were armed with *Davids* spirit and fortitude, what *Gyant* were able to stand before him? *But* if his whole strength consisteth in wording and facing onely, *Quid prodest Simiæ, si videatur esse Leo* [c]? What can it availe an Ape, to conceive himselfe to bee as strong as a Lion? But passing by this vaine ostentation, let us take the matter delivered by him, into examination.

1 He censureth a moderne Writer, for affirming, that the Bishops of the Church, are Guides to the inferiour Clergy, to direct them in matters of Religion.

2 He disputeth against this Position in manner following: *The Pope is not infallible; Ergo,*
the

the Bishops being *Veines of the Body, whereof the Pope is Head*, cannot be Iudges or Guides, to instruct the inferiour Clergy.

3 He saith, that the Author, whom he opposeth, is guided with a *Papall spirit*.

Now this (as I conceive) is the Summe and marrow of the *Dialogaster* his argumentation.

In answer hereunto, the Bishop saith: *that if this Objecter had intended to proceed in a right method of Disputation, he must first of all have stated the Question, and considered what Iudiciall power the Bishops of the Church of England challenge concerning regulating and deciding matters of Controversie, in Religion: and then he might have framed Arguments, made Inferences, and used his Invectives, and Declamations, and not before.* But being bold and blinde, and not regarding and considering the Churches Tenet, concerning Episcopall power, he disputeth in a rude and *deriding* manner; rather *venting his malice against the Order of Bishops* (as Hereticks ⸀ in ancient times were wont to do) than delivering any thing true, substantiall, or to the purpose.

1 The Question is, whether Bishops lawfully called and qualified, according to *the Apostles rule,* 1 *Tim.* 3. have any power of judicature, in matters belonging to Religion, or in questions Theologicall.

2 Whether they be *Veines of the Pope,* and guided by a *Papall spirit,* if they challenge or exercise any such power.

3 Whether they can have no such power, unlesse

c Cyprian. *l* 3 *Ep.* 9 Hæc sunt initia Hæreticorum, & ortus atque conatus Schismaticoru, male cogitantium, ut sibi placeant, & præpositum superbo tumore contemnint.

(20)

less they be endued with Divine Grace, *Ex opere operato.*

Now to these Questions, our Answer is:

1. That Bishops lawfully called, and qualified according to the Apostles Rule, *have a ministeriall and subordinate power,* and authority to determine Theologicall Controversies, *by the Rule of holy Scripture, and by the consentient Tradition* and testimony of the ancient and orthodoxall Catholike Church. For, *Timothy* and *Titus* being Bishops lawfully ordained [b], exercised such power in the Church [c]. *The Bishops and Fathers* in the foure first generall Councels [d] did the like. So likewise did S. *Cyprian,* S. *Augustine,* S. *Irenæus,* S. *Athanasius,* and all other orthodoxall Bishops in their times: *and* the inferiour Clergie, and other Christian people submitted themselves unto them.

[footnote: ...eters oportet obaudire, quicunq; cum Episcopatus successione, cha... accepterunt. d. Euseb *ex Conc. l. 3. c. 18.* Quicquid in Synodis Episcopo... ...his decretum ad universum divinæ voluntati debet attribui.]

2. To enable Bishops to exercise this power of judicature, in such manner as they assume it, it is not necessary, that they be endowed with *miraculous inspiration,* as the Holy Apostles were: *but they* may attain ability to perform this by diligent study, and meditation of holy Scripture, and of the learned writings of the godly fathers, and by helps of good learning, and by the assistance of ordinary grace: *And* this appeareth by the Bishops in the Councels of *Nice, Constantinople, Ephesus,* and *Chalcedon,* and by *Irenæus, Cyprian, Ambrose, Augustine,*

Augustine, Athanasius, Hilarius, Cyrillus, &c.

Thirdly, The **Romane** *Pontife* claimeth a twofold power of judicature, in questions Theologicall: 1. Such an infallible, unerring, and binding power, as that no Church or Creature may appeale from his sentence or Tribunall in any case whatsoever. But the Bishops of the Church of England challenge no such power: *but* they maintaine, that the inferiour Clergie, or any other Christian people, upon waightie and substantiall grounds of veritie, may dissent from their sentence [b]. 2. *The* Pope groundeth the infallibility of his sentence, upon immediate divine inspiration, and because He is the supreme visible head of the universall Catholicke Church, succeeding Saint *Peter*, not only as a Bishop, but as an Apostle [c]. *But* the Bishops in our Church, make not themselves *Apostles*, but are called to be Pastors of the Church, by ordinary meanes, and likewise they attaine ability of true and right judgement by ordinary helpes of learning, and by ordinary assistance of divine Grace.

c Apud *Gratian.* dist. 19 Sic omnes sanctiones Apostolicae sedis, tanquam ipsius divina voce Petri firmatae. Aug. Triumph. Sum. de pot. Eccles. q. 6. ar. 1. Sententia Papae, & sententia Dei est una. Ib. quaest. 18. n. 4. Papa quantum ad cognitionem gratuitam revelatam, est major Angelis. Gretzer. def. Bellar. to. 1. c. 1. Id solum pro verbo Dei veneramur & suscipimus, quod nobis Pontifex ex cathedra Petri, tanquam supremus Christianorum magister, omnium controversiarum judex, definiendo proponit. Guihelm. Rubeo. 4. dist. 19 qu. 2. Papa Christi vicarius, habet tantam potestatem in spiritualibus, quantam habuit Christus, non ut Deus, sed ut homo verus.

Now if it shall be objected, that the inferiour Clergie, and many other good Christians, may equall Bishops, and sometimes exceed them in Learning

(22)

Learning, Piety, Vertue, and therefore Bishops may not be judges of the interiour Clergie.

Our Answer is, 1. *That* by the lawes of our kingdome, and the Canons of our Church, many learned Persons are appointed to be Assistants unto Bishops; and in our *Nationall Synods* (in which all waighty matters concerning Religion are determined) nothing is or may bee concluded, *but by the common Vote and consent of the Major part of the Convocation, which* consisteth of many other learned Divines, besides Bishops.

Secondly, to the end that order may bee observed, discord prevented, and Heresies condemned; it is necessary, that there bee a power of judicature, in some able and worthy persons: *and* our State walking in the way of *pious Antiquity* [a], hath setled this power *in the Bishops of our Church: for* it it shall bee left free, to every singular, and private person, to frame a rule of faith, and to judge and determine matters of Religion, and Theologicall questions and Controversies, by his owne private skill and spirit, *it will* then be consequent, that there shall bee no common Ecclesiasticall rule of faith to settle unity in Religion, *but the people of the land will be divided into as many Sects and factions, as themselves please* [b]: *and* a greater confusion must be among

Christians,

[a] Cyprian *Epist.* 27. Inde per temporum & successionum vices, episcoporum ordinatio, & Ecclesiæ ratio decurrit ut Ecclesia super episcopos constituatur, & omnis actus ecclesiæ per eosdem præpositos gubernetur. Aug. *Epist.* 86. Episcopo tuo noli resistere, & quod ipse facit, sine ullo scrupulo, vel disceptatione, sequere. Hieron. ad Nepotian. Esto subjectus pontifici tuo, & qu[a]si animæ parentem suscipe. Id. ad Luciferian. Ecclesiæ salus in summi sacerdotis dignitate pendet: cui si non exors quædam, & ab omnibus eminens detur potestas, tot in Ecclesiis efficientur schismata, quot sacerdotes

[b] Cyprian. *E. Lep.* 2. Neq; aliunde hæreses abortæ sunt, aut nata sunt schismata, quam inde, quod sacerdoti non obtemperatur: Nec unus in Ecclesia ad tempus sacerdos, & ad tempus judex vice Christi cogitatur, cui secundum magisteria divina obtemperaret fraternitas universa. Idem li 4 *ep.* 9 Unde schismata & hæreses abortæ sunt, nisi dum episcopus qui unus est, & ecclesiæ præest, superba quorundam præsumptione contemnitur, & homo dignatione Dei honoratus ab indignis hominibus judicatur?

Christians, than there was in old time, among Pagans and Infidels.

Lastly, it appeareth by the forme of making and consecrating Bishops, Priests, and Deacons, authorized in this kingdome, that the inferiour Clergy are obliged to submit themselves, to the Bishop, being their Ordinary, and to whom the charge and government is committed over them.

The words of the booke of Ordination, are these which follow:

BISHOP.

Will you reverently obey your Ordinary, and other chiefe Ministers, unto whom the government and charge is committed over you, following with a glad minde and will, their godly admonitions, and submitting your selves to their godly judgements?

Answer:

I will so doe, the Lord being my helper.

Having thus farre proceeded in declaring both the quality of *Episcopall authority*, in judging the inferiour Clergie; *and* also how necessary it is, for preservation of verity and unity in Religion, *that* this authority be respected and maintained: *In* the next place we will examine the waight of the *Dialogaster's* objections.

Object. 1. *If Bishops are to be guides to the inferiour Clergie, in matters of Religion: then the inferiour Clergie, must lay their hands on their mouth; and be altogether regulated by their Dictates. But this is unreasonable,* &c.

Answ. No such thing will follow: for although the inferiour Clergie are to be guided by

the

the Bishops in matters of Religion, so farre as the Bishops instruct them, according to the common rule of faith collected out of *Holy Scripture*, and confirmed by the Vote of *Primitive Antiquity*, and which is approved and ratified *by the Church*, whereof they are members: *yet* they are not absolutely or altogether to be directed by the Bishops; for they have liberty to dissent, *if by* waighty and substantiall arguments they shall be able to demonstrate, *that the Bishops determination, or doctrine is repugnant to Orthodoxall Verity* [a].

But now againe on the contrary, *if* any of the inferiour Clergie proceed (as the *Dialogaster* hath done,) *and be able to produce nothing* waighty, effectuall, firme, or solid, *but that which is meerely schismaticall, declamatory, and verball: Then* here is just cause, that the inferiour Clergie, in due obedience, should submit themselves to *Episcopall* sounder judgement.

Object. 2. *A Bishops Rotchet cannot conferre Grace, ex opere operato:* Ergo, *The inferiour Clergie are not bound to submit themselves to the Bishops judgement*, &c.

Ansiv. The ground of this objection is apparently false: *for* if inferiours are not bound to submit themselves to the judgement of any, but of such only as have received extraordinary grace *ex opere operato* [b], *Then* it wil be consequent, that *Parochians* are not obliged to submit themselves to the instruction of their godly and lawfull Pastors: *Neither* are Children bound to submit themselves to their Parents directions, because

cause holy order, and paternity conferre not extraordinary grace to Priests, or to Parents, *ex opere operato*, to instruct their Parochians, or their Children, as the Holy Prophets and Apostles instructed the Church, to wit, by a miraculous power of inspiration.

Object. 3. *Bishops have not such infallibility as the Pope challengeth: for we deny the Popes infallibility, or that it can convey it selfe as from the Head, and confine it selfe within the Veines of the body of the Prelacy. Ergo the inferiour Clergy are not bound to submit themselves to the Bishops judgement.*

Answ. 1. If none may instruct and guide others in matters of Religion, but they onely, which have such infallibility, as *the Pope* claimeth [a], and is conveyed from him as the head, into them as Veines : *Then* neither Saint *Augustine*, nor any other of the Fathers, nor any other man since the Apostles, might guide and instruct others in matters of Religion: for none of these had such infallibility, as the Pope challengeth, *&c.*

Secondly, If none may be guides to others in things Divine and Religious, but such only as have the same infallibility which the *Pope* claimeth : How comes it to passe, that *the Author of this Dialogue*, having neither *extraordinary wit nor wealth of learning*, presumeth to make himselfe a Iudge [b], and Instructor of others, not only in his owne Cure, but of all men, learned, and unlearned in the kingdome [c]: *and if any man vary (as all Wise men doe)* from his placits contained in cer-

a Aug. Triumph. *Sum. de potest. Ecclef* q.6.ar.1. Nullus potest appellare à Papa ad Deum, quia una sentencia est, & una Curia Dei & Papæ.
b H. B. *Treat of privat devot. praef. I heare, alas, poor Burto he is crackt: discontentment, or hope of preferment have embarked him in this perilous adventare : What shall I say? Am I crackt? Wherewith? Not. I am sure, either with too much learning (as* Festus *charged* Paul) *or too much living : And if I am mad, I am not the first.*
c *Cyprian. ad Iubaian* Novatianus similarum more, quæ cum homines non sint, homines imitentur, vult ecclesiæ catholicæ authoritatem vendicare, quando ipse in ecclesia non sit.

taine irregular, and unlicenfed *Pamphlets*. *Hee forth-with ftigmatizeth them* d *in print, threatneth to publifh Books in Latine againft them, He turnes* White into Blacke e, *He cafteth durt in their faces,* f *and flings about with his heeles, like a netled Iade.*

Now what partiality is this, *to make the Reverend, and learned Bifhops* of the Church, *Veines of the Pope, becaufe* they by lawfull authority guide and inftruct the Clergie, fubject to their Epifcopall jurifdiction: *and* in the meane time that this *Scripturient*, having received no authority from God or men, and being deftitute of all abilities for fo great a worke, fhould conftitute himfelfe a *Iudge Paramount*, even in the moft profound, and obfcure queftions of Theologie g.

d Hier. Apol.c. Ruff. Quicunq; te offenderit, quamvis fimplex, quamvis innoxius fit, ilico fiet criminofus.
e Plea To the Appeale pag. 5. The Puritans ftick not to caft him (D. Wh) in the teeth with, White died backe.
f Tertul. e. Hermog. Maledicere fingulis, officium bonæ confcientiæ judicat.
g Greg. Nazian. Apolog. fuga: ftulte, temereque faciunt, qui priusquam ipfi fatis doctrina inftructi funt, aliorum fe magiftros prohtentur, Figlinamq; (ut vulgo dici folet) in dolio difcunt.

✥✥✥✥✥✥✥✥✥✥✥✥✥✥✥✥✥✥✥

A. Brother, fuch a refolution had need have a good ground to ftand upon: and being a matter of fuch moment, it requires our beft zeale & ftrength, efpecially to vindicate *the Doctrine of our Reverend Mother the Church of England*, which wee have fucked from her purer Breafts, nor onely fo, but to vindicate her name from reproach: *for* if it be fo as you have faid, that the Doctrine of our Church is by that book overthrown, then confequently (as I conceive)

conceive) she must deepely suffer, and be wounded through the sides of those, whom he so often in his Book brandeth with the odious name of *Novell Sabbatarians*.

B. Brother, you conceite aright; *for* in truth, all those Calumnious, and odious Termes which he gives to those, whose opinions (except *Brabournes* only) he impugneth in his Treatise; *as venomous Serpents, Noysome Tares, Pestilent weedes, and Vncleane Beasts* (termes to bee abhorred of all true Christians) and in a word *Novell Sabbatarians, they all result upon our deare Mother the Church of England* c. *For* who are the most of those, or rather all, whom he thus stigmatizeth? are they not, or were they not in their time, the true-bred Children of the Church of Engl. all unanimously professing, and maintaining her Orthodox Doctrines? *Can* therefore the Mother be free, when her pious Sons are so traduced and reproached, and that for defending those very doctrines, which by her means they sucked from the breasts of both the Testaments:

A. That must needs follow, I confesse.

c *With lye and all*

Answ.

(28)

Answ. In the former declamatory passage, these particulars following are to be observed.

1 The *hypocrisie* [a] of this Declamitant, who professeth himselfe an obedient Son to his deare and reverend Mother, the Church of *England*: whereas in the precedent Section, he most contemptuously disgraceth *Episcopal Authority* ordain'd by the holy Apostles, and established in the Ch. of *England* ever since the reformation; accounting the *Prelates* (if they exercise that power of judicature wch the Church of *England* approveth, as being descended from Primitive and Apostolicall Ordination) Vines of the *Pope*. And more than so, *This* Dialogue-broacher [b] in other Pamphlets declares himselfe to be an adversary to the Ecclesiasticall policy, Rites, Ceremonies, and Canons of our present Church: and scarce any professed Schismatick of later dayes hath intreated conformable persons of good quality with more despitefull abuses, than this hypocrite (who stileth himselfe an obedient Sonne of his Mother the Church) hath done.

[a] August. Serm. in Mont. l.2.c.3. Qui vult videri quod non est, hypocrita est. Id. in Psalm. 103. Paries dealbatus hypocrisis & simulatio: paries dealbatus, foris tectorium, intus lutum. Id. d civ. D. lib. 2. Malignitas Dæmonum, qui alicubi se transfigurat in Angelū Lucis, forum, benegerum deceptoris.

[b] Reade this in his *Treatise*, intituled, *Christs confession and complaint* pag. 50 an. pag. 59. In which he condemneth Episcopall government, saying, It is prohibited by Gods Law, Luc. 22.24.

c.   1 Pet. 5.3. Mat. 20.25. 2 Tim. 2.3, 4. *And he applyes S. Pauls Text*, Col. 2.2). *to the ceremonies of the Church*, pag. 60. *They look too little, but the silencing of such as stumble at their Ceremonies and Hierarchie. To defend the injunctions of men and their unprofitable Hierarchie. Plea. Such kinde of Ministers are not wanting to helpe forward the re-erecting of the Romish Baal in our Land, had they but a yong Manasses to restore the Altars and Groves which good King Ezekiah his Father had pulled downe.*

2 This Dialogist falsely accuseth his Adversary, in laying to his charge, that he hath stigmatized all such as dissent from him in the Question of the Sabbath, *Venomous Serpents, noisome Tares, pestilent Weeds, and uncleane Beasts:* for it is apparent *in Pagina secunda of the Epistle Dedicatory*

tha

that those termes are applyed to notorious Hereticks, malicious Schismaticks, prophane Hypocrites, and proud disturbers of the peace and unity of the Church [c]. The Bishops words are; *This being the condition of the Church militant, it cannot be otherwise, but that in all ages there shall be found among those which professe Christ, not only such as are vertuous and sound in faith, but also men of corrupt minds, and reprobate, concerning the faith: Venomous Serpents, noisome Tares, pestilent Weeds* [d], *and uncleane beasts. Our Saviours owne prediction was; There shall arise false Prophets, &c. S. Paul, Oportet Hæreses esse, &c.*

[c] Hieron. *apolog.* e Ruff. Tu nimium suspitiosus & querulus, qui dicta in Hereticos, ad tuam refers contumeliam.

[d] Idem e. Luciferian. Non solum in Ecclesia morantur oves, nec mundæ tantū aves volitant, sed frumentum in agro seritur, & inter nitentia culta Lappaq; & tribuli & steriles dominantur avenæ.

"3 Another branch of *Br. B.* his Declamation,
"is: *The Bishop in his booke brandeth those
"whose opinions he impugneth, with the odious
"name of Novell Sabbatarians.*

"Our answer is: 1. The Bishop in his Treatise
"brandeth not all such as dissent from him in his
"Tenet of the *Sab.* &c. with that name: neither
"brandeth he any therewith, because they teach
"Christian people to observe the Lord's-day
"religiously, and to spend the same in the perfor-
"mance of holy and spirituall duties, so far as is
"necessary for their godly edification, and in
"such manner as the Canon and Precept of the
"Christian Church hath enjoyned: for he hol-
"deth this to be a necessary duty obliging al good
"Christians.

"2 He giveth this Title and Name very just-
"ly to all those, who proudly and peremptorily
"maintaine the maine Principles and Positions,
"upon which Sabbatarian Hereticks in ancient
"and

"and in moderne times have grounded their er-
"rour, touching the necessary observation of the
"old legall Sabbath.

"The Reader shall finde these Principles and
"Positions peremptorily taught for divine truth
"(by those Teachers whose opinions the Bishop
"impugneth) layed downe in his Treatise, *Page*
"20. *&c.*

"*The observation of the Seventh day, and also the*
"*precise resting from worldly affaires, is morall; nei-*
"*ther is there any thing in the fourth Commande-*
"*ment that might intimate it to be Ceremoniall.*

"*The 4th Commandement can be no more partly*
"*morall, & partly Ceremoniall, than the same living*
"*creature can be partly a Man, and partly a beast.*

"*The fourth Commandement is part of the Law of*
"*Nature, and thus part of the Image of God, and is*
"*no more capable of a Ceremony, than God himselfe.*

"*The fourth Commandement, in every part there-*
"*of, as it is contained in the Decalogue, is morall, and*
"*of the Law of Nature.*

"*The Decalogue being the same with the Law of*
"*Nature, is one, and the same for ever: it followeth*
"*necessarily, that the Sabbath being a part of that*
"*Decalogue, is to remaine for ever.*

"*The observation of the seventh day is of the Law*
"*of Nature: it was established before Christ was pro-*
"*mised, and therefore it is not ceremoniall, but of the*
"*Law of nature, and perpetuall.*

"The Summe and substance of the former Po-
"sitions is: The fourth Commandement of the
"Decalogue, is purely, intirely, and totally mo-
"rall; it is a Precept of the Law of Nature, and
"O

"of the same quality, both for morality and per-
"petuity with other Commandements of the
"Law of Nature, neither was there any thing Ce-
"remoniall in it.

"Now the judicious Reader will presently
"observe, that the *Sabbatarian Heresie*, concerning
"the perpetuall observation of the old Legall
"Sab. is a necessary and undeniable Conclusion,
"issuing out of the former Positions.

"For every Law or Precept, purely, intirely,
"and totally morall, is perpetuall and unchange-
"able: the same must be intirely observed; and
"if nothing *positive or Ceremoniall be found therein,*
"*then no branch* or member thereof can cease or
"be omitted.

"But the keeping holy of the *Seventh day Sab-*
"*bath*, namely Saturday, was a maine part of the
"fourth Commandement; for it was the Subject
"or materiall Object of that Commandement,
"literally, expressely, and positively specified
"and commanded by God Almighty in the De-
"calogue.

"Therefore from the Premises it will be con-
"sequent, that the Seventh day Sabbath, being
"Saturday, must be kept holy untill the end of
"the world.

"The first Proposition is confirmed in manner
"following.

"*The prime, speciall, and expresse materiall Ob-*
"*ject of every Law, is a substantiall part of that Law:*
"and it is of the same kinde and quality with the
"Law it selfe: and therefore if the Law be intire-
"ly and naturally morall, then the expresse and
"speciall

" speciall object of the same, is of the same qua-
" lity.

"For example, in the fifth Commandement
" of the Decalogue, *Honour thy father and thy mo-*
" *ther, &c.* Naturall Parents are the prime,
" speciall, and expresse Object of that Law
" therefore although other Objects may be ad
" ded, as *honour the King; give honour to Presbyter*
" *that rule well; honour Masters, &c.* Yet natu
" rall Father and Mother being named, expressed
" and specified in the Commandement, remain
" indelible, because they are the prime Object
" thereof.

"In like manner, if the fourth Commande
" ment were naturall and intirely morall, like un
" to the fifth: then the particular day expresse
" and described therein, namely Saturday, mu
" be observed, although the Apostles and Chr
" stian Church might adde the Lord's-day an
" some other Festivals, for the enlarging of th
" service of Christ.

"4 The Bishop also in his Treatise, 235. &
" 249. &c. hath observed certaine desperate pa
" sages in those mens Sermons and Tractat
" whom he stileth *Novell Sabbatarians*: to wit,

" *To doe any servile worke or businesse upon t*
" *Lord's-day, is as great a sinne, as to kill a man,*
" *to commit adultery.*

" *To throw a Bowle on the Sabbath-day, is as gre*
" *a sinne, as to kill a man: And to make a Feast*
" *Wedding-dinner on the Lord's day, is as great a si*
" *as for a father to take a knife and cut his child*
" *throat.*

"*To ring more Bels than one upon the Lord's-day*
"*to call the People to Church, is as great a sin as to*
"*commit murder.*

"*In Harvest time, though the Corne be in danger,*
"*yet better were it for us that it should rot on the*
"*ground, than for us by carrying it in with the breach*
"*of the Sabbath, to treasure up unto our selves wrath,*
"*&c.*

"*It is not lawfull for people to go out of their hou-*
"*ses to walke in the fields.*

"These former Dictats are borrowed from
"the old *Pharisees*; and the moderne Authors
"who have revived and maintained them, com-
"ply herein with *Sabbatarian Hereticks*.

"Thus to satisfie my judicious Reader, I have
"delivered the reasons inducing me to stile cer-
"taine new Scripturients and Predicants, whose
"opinions I impugned, *Novell Sabbatarians*: and
"if *Br. B.* and his Allies are offended, and hold
"this Title odious, let them right themselves;
"not by raging, and thrusting out *rayling and li-*
"*belling Pamphlets, marching up and downe in blew*
"*Iackets*: but by renouncing and recanting those
"scandalous Positions, which are apt to impoy-
"son Christian People with Iudaical and Sabba-
"tarian heresie.

5 Those persons which the Bishop intended, when he us'd that terme of *Novell Sabbatizers*, were so far from being the true bred children of the Church of *England*, that they were either in heart, or in open profession adheres to the *Presby-terian Policy*; and they sucked not their Doctrine of the Sabbath from the breasts of both the Te-

F   staments;

ſtaments, *but* partly from the corrupt Fountaines of Ancient Heretickes, *and* partly out of the broken Cesternes of their owne private fancies.

B. The Doctrine of the Church of England, concerning the Sabbath, is *moſt clearely* ᵃ, and fully ſet forth in the Booke of Homilies: which Booke the 35. Article (to which all we Miniſters doe ſubſcribe) doth commend, as containing *A godly and wholeſome Doctrine, and neceſſary for theſe times, and* therefore judged to be read in Churches, by the Miniſters diligently, and diſtinctly, that they may be underſtood of the People.

Anſw. The Homily ſetteth forth the Doctrine of the Church of England, *if the words and ſentences thereof, be rightly expounded:* to wit, according to the rule of the Scripture, the common vote and conſentient teſtimony of the Orthodox-all Catholike Church of Chriſt in all ages, and the precedent and ſubſequent Lawes, Statutes, and Canons of the kingdome and Church of England. But if the words and ſentences thereof be not *rightly expounded* ᵇ, according to the foreſaid rules, but according to mens private interpretation,

ᵃ If *Br. Aſotus* had ſaid clearely, and *left out the word* moſt, *he had ſaid* more, *than he could have made good.*

ᵇ Tertul. d. præſcript. ca. 17. Tantum veritati obſtrepit adulter ſenſus, quantum & corruptor ſtilus.

tation, then the same may bee a meanes, to lead people into error: for so it fareth sometimes even with holy Scripture it selfe c.

2 Some passages in the Homily are *ambiguous*. Therefore the doctrine of the Church of England is not *most clearely* set forth in the same.

The Antecedent is proved by these Instances.

The Homily saith: *As for the time which Almighty God hath appointed his people to assemble together solemnly, it doth appeare by the fourth Commandement of God, Remember thou keepe holy the Sabbath day. Vpon which day, it is plaine in the Acts of the Apostles, ca. 13. the people accustomably resorted together, and heard diligently the Law, and the Prophets read among them.*

c Hieron. *Com. in Eph.* 1. Interpretatione perversa, ex Evangelio Domini fit Evangelium hominis, & quod pejus est, Diaboli. *Id. c. Lucifer.* Nec sibi blandiantur, si de scripturarū capitulis videntur sibi affirmare quod dicunt, cū & diabolus de scripturis aliqua sit locutus: & scripturæ non in legendo consistunt, sed in intelligendo.

In this passage the Homily might seeme, to those who maintaine the Saturday Sabbath, to make that day, a weekly festivall: because the Apostles, upon that day, even after Christs Ascension, entred into Synagogues, and did there performe Christian religious offices, *Act.* 13. 14, 44. and *Chap.* 17. 2.

It followeth in the Homily: *God doth not binde Christians so straightly to observe the utter Ceremonies of the Sabbath, in forbearing of work and labour in time of great necessity.*

In this passage the Homily hath not clearely, and explicitely declared. 1. How farre forth the Sabbath of the fourth Commandement was Ceremoniall. 2. What kinde of worke, and labour in particular, Christians may lawfully use upon the Holy day.

Br. B. pag. 22. Will admit no work or labour

F 2 upon

upon the Sunday, but such only as is of absolute necessity, as in time of *Scar-fire, invasion of enemies*, &c. But the Ancient Imperiall lawes permitted sundry workes of lesse necessity than the former upon the Sunday, *pag. 219.* and grave Divines, as *Calvin, Bucer, Beza*, &c. approve the same.

[marginal note:] a Videtur de ... pag. 149 Non vi denius im; solum quod pad concilium Arelatense, Constantinus in suis constitutionibus, tempore pluvio, aut alio necessitatis casu, permittit ut messes, aut vindemiæ, etiam die Dominico colligantur. Quia si ad famis propriæ solutium, licuit Discipulis sabbato aristas vellere: Cur non liceat in tali casu ad pulsionem & præventionem famis communis, terram còserere, & messem aut vindemiam sibi are. Bez. in Cantic. Ho.30. Ut autem Christiani, eo die a suis quotidianis laboribus abstinerent, præter id temporis quod in cœtu ponebatur: Id neq; illis Apostolicis temporibus mandatum, neq; prius fuit imperatum, quam id ab Imperatoribus Christianis, neque à rerum sanctarum meditatione abstraheretur, neq; ita præside sancitum est.

It seemes therefore, that the Homily hath not most clearely, and fully declared all things necessary to be knowne, touching this question.

Againe, the Homily saith: *Whatsoever is found in the fourth Commandement, appertaining to the Law of Nature, as a thing most godly, most just, and needfull for the setting forth of God's glory, it ought to be retained of all good Christians.*

Out of the former words it may be collected, that nothing in the fourth Commandement is simply morall, and of the Law of Nature, but that which is most godly, most just, and necessary for the setting forth of Gods glory: And if this be the sence of the Homily (as no doubt it is) then the fourth Commandement is not in force according to the letter, but only according to the equity and Analogie thereof.

Lastly the Homily saith: *God hath given expresse charge to all men, that upon the Sabbath Day, which is now our Sunday, they should cease from all weekely,*

weekely, and worke-day labour: and God doth command the observation of this Holy day: and we must be carefull to keep the Sabbath day, which is the Sunday.

Out of the former passage, these questions arise. 1. What the Homily intendeth, in saying, *God hath given expresse charge* &c. *and God hath commanded,* &c. Whether God hath immediately, by any Divine Law, *expressely commanded* the Observation of Sunday? and in what Texts of Scripture this Law and Commandement, touching Sunday, is to be found? Or whether the meaning of the Homily is not, that God hath thus commanded Christians, by a mediate or ministeriall Law, and precept of his Church.

It may bee questioned likewise, in what sence the Homily stileth the Sunday, *the Sabbath day:* whether in a proper and literall sence, according to the stile of the old Law: or *in a mysticall and analogicall sence,* as Christ is called our Passeover, 1 Cor. 5. 7.

Now from the precedent observations, it is consequent, that the Doctrine of the Church of England is not *most clearly,* or so plainly and expressely set forth in the Homily, as this Objector pretendeth when he saith, *pag.* 13. *The words of the Homily, as you have heard, and every one may plainely see, are so expresse, cleare, and full, that they cannot possibly admit the least ambiguity.*

Reasons to the contrary. 1. *Evidens conscri solet illud, quod ita sufficienter movet intellectum, ut in libera hominis potestate non sit dissentire* [a]*:* That onely is to be reputed cleare and evident, which in such sort affecteth the understanding, that it is

Aqu. Scot. Greg. Valent. Fr. alij Scholast. Doctores.
Aug. c. Crescon. Gram. li. 3. Ipse sententia loquitur, cujus verba sic fulgent, ut si eam velis abscondere, quantumlibet tenebrarum latebras, sui nimio splendore perrumperet.

not in the free power of an intelligent Person to dissent from it. But this definition, of cleare and evident, cannot bee applyed to the words of the Homily, for the reasons before delivered.

2. According to *Tertullian*.[b] *Sententiæ et definitiones, quarum est aperta natura, aliter quam sonant, non sapiunt*: Sentences and Definitions which are cleare and evident, cannot be expounded otherwise than as the words sound.

[b] Tertul. d. Re-
sur Carnu. ca 33.

But the words of the Homily, concerning the Sabbath, which this Objector produceth, doe neither force the understanding of every intelligent Reader to yeeld assent *to Br. B. his Exposition*: and unlesse wee expound them otherwise, than the words seeme to sound, we shall fall into many absurdities.

Ergo. It is false, which the Objector delivereth, to wit, *The words of the Homily are so expresse, cleare, and plainely delivered, as that they cannot admit the least Question or Ambiguity*.

✠✠✠✠✠✠✠✠✠✠✠✠✠✠✠✠✠✠✠✠

B. The Homily of the time and place of prayer, *part first*, sheweth, That our Lord's Day is grounded upon the fourth Commandement of the Decalogue, in these words: *Whatsoever is contained in the Commandement appertaining to the Law of Nature, as a thing most godly, most just and needefull*

for

for the setting forth of Gods glory, it ought to be retained and kept of all good Christian people: and therefore by this Commandement we ought to have a time, *as* one day in the weeke, wherein we ought to rest, yea from our lawfull, and needfull workes.

For like as it appeareth by this Commandement, that no man in the sixe dayes, ought to be slothfull, or idle, but diligently to labour in that state wherein God hath set him: even so GOD hath given expresse charge to all men, that upon the Sabbath day, which is now our Sunday, they should cease from all weekely and worke day labour; to the intent, that like as God Himselfe wrought sixe dayes, and rested the Seventh, and blessed, and sanctified, and consecrated it to quietnesse, and rest from labour; even so God's obedient People should use the Sunday holily, and rest from their common and daily businesse, and also give themselves wholly to heavenly exercises of God's true Religion and Service.

So that God doth not onely command the Observation of this Holy Day, *but* also by his own example doth stir and provoke
us

us to the diligent keeping of the same. Good natural children wil not only becom obedient to the Commandement of their Parents, but also have a diligent eye to their doings, and gladly follow the same ¡ So if we will bee the children of our Heavenly Father, wee must be carefull to keepe the Christian Sabbath Day, which is the Sunday, not only for that it is God's expresse Commandement, but also to declare our selves to bee loving children in following the example of our Gracious Lord and Father.

Againe thus it may plainely appeare, that God's will and Commandement was to have a solemne time, and standing day in the week, wherein the People should come together, and have in remembrance his wonderfull benefits, and to render Him thankes for them, as appertaineth to loving, kind and obedient People. *This example and Commandement of God the godly Christian people began to follow immediately after the Ascension of our Lord Christ, &c. So the Homily, and much more*, whence we plainely observe these conclusions. 1 That

1 That all Christians ought, and are bound in conscience of the fourth Commandement, to keep the Lord's-day holily.

2 That by the force of the fourth Commandement, one day in seven is perpetually to be kept holy.

3 That the keeping of the Lord's-day is grounded upon, and commanded in the fourth Commandement, and so is not of humane institution.

4 That the Lord's-day is, and may bee called our Christian Sabbath-day, therefore it is not Iewish to call it so.

5 That this Day is wholly to be spent in holy rest and duties of sanctification; *and therefore* no part of it to be spent in vaine pleasures, and prophane pastimes.

Now *the Author* of the Treatise doth overthrow all these conclusions: for *page* 23. his words are: *This Position (to wit, that the fourth Commandement is properly and perpetually morall, and is for quality and obligation equall to the other nine Commandements,* which for many yeares hath raigned in Pamphlets, Pulpits, and Conventicles, and is entertained as an Oracle, by all such as either

ther openly professe, or doe leane towards the disciplinarian faction) is destitute of truth.

These are his words: *which comparing with the words of the Homily of our Church already cited, are found quite contrary. For the Homily saith: That the fourth Commandement is a Law of Nature*, and ought to be retained and kept of all good Christians, in as much as it commandeth one day of the Weeke for rest: and God hath given an expresse charge to all Men, that the Sabbath-day, which is our Sunday, should be spent wholly in heavenly exercises of God's true Religion and Service.

Answ. The Summe of the former accusation is, *That the Bishop in his Treatise overthrowes the Doctrine of the Church of England in the point of the Sabbath: For his Doctrine is repugnant to the Homily, &c. which teacheth that the fourth Commandement is of the Law of Nature, &c. and that all Christians ought to keep it holily: and one day in seven is perpetually to be kept holy: the keeping of the Lord's-day is commanded by the 4th Commandement: The Lord's-day may be called the Christian Sabbath-day. Lastly, the Lord's-day ought wholly to be spent in holy rest, and duties of sanctification.* Now

Now the Bishop (saith the Objector) hath opposed all these positions, for he hath affirmed in his Treatise of the Sabbath: that *the fourth Commandement is not properly, intirely, and perpetually morall, like as are the other nine:* and he hath permitted some bodily exercise and recreation; to wit, such as is honest and sober, upon the Sunday: and hee denies, that in a legall sense the Lord's-day is to be called the Sabbath-day.

To the former, the *Bishops* answer is; that the Objector hath *snatched some words of the Homily, but he hath not duly observed the true sense* and meaning thereof [a].

For first, the Homily doth not affirme, that *the fourth Commandement is purely, intirely, and properly morall, and of the Law of Nature, like as are the other nine.* But that *whatsoever is found in the Commandement appertaining to the Law of Nature, being most godly, most just, and needfull to the setting forth of Gods glory, ought to be retained.*

Now if nothing else in the fourth Commandement is of the Law of Nature, but only that which is most just, godly, and needfull to the setting forth of Gods glory: then the *Homily* maketh not the letter of that Commandement of the Law of nature: *but* the intent and meaning thereof is, That the fourth Commandement, in respect of the naturall equity [b] (which is, that *the Rulers of the Church must appoint necessary convenient, and sufficient time for Divine Worship, and for religious offices*,) is morall, and of the Law of Nature.

And if the Objector will straine the words of
the

Athanas. Orat. 1. c. Arrian. Verba quidem profert, veram tamen inde sententiam suffa-ratur. Tertul. ad Praxean. Malo te ad sensum rei quā ad sonum vocabuli exerceas.

b Al. Hal 3. q.31. m 5 ar 1. Hoc præ-cepto præcipitur tempus vacationis aliquod, & secundum hoc est mo-rale legis naturæ, & hoc secundum tempus determinatum p̄ se tempore gratiæ

(43)

G 2

(44)

the Homily to a further sense, let him well consider, into what absurdities and contradictions he will be forced to plunge himselfe.

For *if this Commandement be intirely, purely, and properly Morall* [a], *and of the Law of Nature*, like as the other nine: Then *it must have all the essentiall characters of the Law of Nature, and of Precepts purely, and entirely morall*: But it wanteth all these, as is proved by demonstrative arguments in the Bishops book, *pag. 26. untill pag. 37.* and *pag. 172.*

Neverthelesse, that I may more fully discover the ignorance and presumption of this Dialogist, I shall propound an argument against him, which he will hardly be able to solve, to wit:

The Law of Nature was made knowne to all mankinde [b] *by the Common light of naturall reason: The same is immutable, unchangeable* [c], *eternall, indispensible.*

But the fourth Commandement concerning the Sabbath was not imprinted naturally, or made knowne to all mankinde by the common light of naturall reason: *but it was made knowne only and wholly, by divine and supernaturall revelation.* *Also* the fourth Commandement was changeable and mutable: for the Sabbath of that Commandement, which was Saturday (according to the Objectors owne Tenet) was changed into Sunday: *And* lastly it admitted sundry dispensations, *pag. 34. 67.*

Now the premises being indubitate Verities, *The* conclusion is firme, to wit, *That the fourth Commandement of the Decalogue, is no precept*

---

[a] *B. Gosp. and Law recon. p. 58. The Comandement of the Sabbath is morall, and so non tempi perpetuall then all the rest: for if some of the rest of the Comandements be abolished, then neither the fourth. Pag. 4. & 49. The Law of the Sabbath was imprinted in Adams heart by the Law of Nature.*

[b] *Justin. Etimol. l. 5. ca. 4. Jus naturale commune est omnium nationum, eo quod ubiq; instinctu naturæ, non constitutione aliqua habetur.*

[c] *Decret. Dist. 5. Naturale jus ab exordio rationalis creaturæ incipit, nec tempore, sed immutabile permanet. Aug. Confess. l. 3. c. 4. Lex scripta in cordibus hominum, quam nec ipsa quidem delet iniquitas.*

cept of the Law of Nature [d]: *neither* is it purely, intirely, and properly morall, like the other nine; *but* meerely positive, in respect of any one particular day of the Weeke specified in the same.

[d] Theod. *in Ezek.* 20. 12. *Illud, non mœchaberis, non furtum facies, & alia cum his conjuncta, alios quoque homines naturæ lex edocuit. At*

Sabbati observandi, non natura magistra, sed latio legis. Walæus & *Alii Synops. purior. Theolog. disp.*21.*n.*20. *Sabbati præceptum non est à naturæ necessitate, ut reliqua præcepta, quæ menti insita, & per se cognita sunt, sed* χτ᾽ συνθήκην, *ex voluntaria Dei institutione.* D. Bound. *d. Sab. l.*1.*p.*11. *Indeed this Law was given in the beginning, not so much by the light of Nature, as the rest of the Commandements were, but by expresse word. For though this be the Law of Nature, that some dayes should be separated to Gods worship, yet that it should be every seventh day, that, the LORD himselfe set downe.*

The Bishop desires to receive some reasonable answer from *Br. B.* to this and to other the like arguments, delivered in his Treatise of the Sabbath: for if he shall (according to his rude manner) barke and blatter against his adversaries Positions, and dissemble his arguments, it is apparent that he maintaines a forlorne and desperate cause.

✦✦✦✦✦✦✦✦✦✦✦✦✦✦✦✦✦✦✦✦

B. The Homily saith: *All Christians ought and are bound in conscience of the fourth Commandement, to keepe the Lord's-day holily.*

Ans. 1. The equity and Analogie of the fourth Commandement, obligeth Christians to observe a convenient and sufficient time for Gods worship and service, and for the exercise of spirituall and religious duties.

2 After such time as the Orthodoxall Catho-like

like Church, hath upon *the example of the holy Apostles* and for other weighty reasons, devoted the Sunday of every Weeke to the exercise of Religious duties, Christian people in obedience to the Law of the Church, grounded upon the equity of the fourth Commandement, and the example of the Apostles, are bound in conscience to observe that Day holily, in the performance of religious duties, *pag.* 100.

B. The Lord's-day is, and may be called our Christian Sabbath-day : and therefore it is not Iewish to call it so.

Answ. 1. The Lord's-day is not the *litterall Sabbath* of the fourth Commandement; and therfore in propriety of speech it cannot be called the Sabbath-day, expressely or in particular commanded in the Decalogue; but the same is stiled by the Homily, our *Christian Sabbath*, in a mysticall and analogicall sense: *even as mortification* is called Circumcision, *Rom* 2.29. *and sincerity and truth*, are called unleavened bread, 1 *Cor.* 8.5.

B. That this day is wholly to be spent in holy rest, and duties of sanctification: and therefore no part of it to be spent in vaine pleasures, and profane pastimes.

Answ.

Ansv. 1. The Homily (according to the Tenet also of other Divines [a]) permitteth *some kinde of labour upon the Sunday*: Therefore, *by wholly*, it understandeth not every houre and minute of the day; but so much thereof, as is necessary and morally sufficient for the performance of the religious duties of the day, *pag.* 218, 219. 225. 231.

[a] Bucer. *in Mat.* 12. p. 113. Eximatur è cordibus hominum opinio necessitatis, ne quis credat eum diem, per se, esse aliis sanctiorem, vel operari in eo, per se esse peccatum. Danæus *lib. Christ. l* 2. *c.* 9. Nobis Christianis, non tanta tamve severa & rigida observatio (ne laboremus in die Dominica) imposita est. Nam ex lege Constantini, licet serere, & metere in die Dominica, si commodum sit. Aquin. 2. 2. *q.* 122. *ar.* 4 *d l.* 4. Non est ita arcta prohibitio operandi in die Dominica, sicut in die Sabbati: sed quædam opera conceduntur in die Dominica, quæ in die Sabbati prohibebantur: sicut decoctio ciborū, &c.

2 If the Objector would have proceeded sincerely, he should have declared, whether by *vaine pleasures, and profane pastimes*, he understandeth all bodily exercise and recreation in generall: or such only as is vitious in quality, or by reason of circumstances, *pag.* 229.

If he meane the first, we finde no words in the Homily, condemning in generall all recreation, to wit, such as is *sober and honest* in quality, and which is not attended with evill circumstances.

But if he understand the Homily in the latter sense, to wit, that it condemneth ungodly pastimes: *Then* he might have observed the Bishops words, *pag.* 258. *The Lawes of our Church and Common-wealth condemne and chastise all things profane and vitious upon the Lord's-day.* And *pag.* 259. *All obscene, lascivious, and voluptuous pastimes are prohibited on this day.* And *pag.* 229. *All kindes of Recreations which are of evill quality in regard of their object: or which are attended with evill circumstances, &c. If they bee used upon the Lord's-*

Lord's-day or on other Festival daies, they are sacrilegious, &c. And in the Ep. Dedicat. *Profanation of the Lords-'day, and of other solemne Festivall dayes which are devoted to religious offices, is impious and hateful in the sight of God and all good men; and therfore to bee avoided, by such as feare God, and to be corrected and punished in those which shall offend,* and pag. 109. 110. *This Ordinance and observation of the Lord's Day, began in the holy Apostles age, and hath universally beene continued ever since, to the great honour of Christ our Saviour, and to the marvellous benefit of Christian soules, who upon that holy day, are edified weekely in godlinesse, vertue, and true Religion. And therefore we justly account all those who maligne the honour of this blessed day, prophane and sacrilegious.*

※※※※※※※※※※※※※※※※※※※

A. The Author seemes to acknowledge some morality naturall, to be in the fourth Commandement: for *pag.* 135. He saith, *Our resting from labour, in respect of the generall, is grounded upon the Law of Nature, or the equity of the fourth Commandement.*

B. This is nothing to the purpose to acquit him from being an Adversary to the expresse doctrine of our Church. *Dolosus versatur in Vniversalibus* (it was the speech of *King Iames.*) The naturall morality of

the

the fourth Commandement, is not in generall, to imply some *Individuum Vagum*, some certaine uncertaine indefinite time for God's Worship [a] : for the Commandement is expresse, for a certaine day in the weeke for the Sabbath Day; *Remember the Sabbath to sanctifie it.* It saith not, remember to set apart and allow some time for the service of God, but it determines the time and day: lest otherwise being left undetermined, man should forget God Himselfe, and allow no time or day at all for God's service; or if he did, God should bee beholden to him for it.

[a] Urfin. Cat. d. Sabba. Non sumus allegati, ut diem vel Iovis, vel Saturni, vel Mercurij, vel ullum alium, certum habeamus. Rivet. *in Exod.* 20. *pag.* 193. Petitur principium, cum id pro confesso sumitur, ad substantiam mandati quarti, quatenus morale est, pertinere circumstantiam diei septimi. Phil. Melancht. *loc. Com. d. 3. præcepto.* Recte dicitur in tertio præcepto duas esse partes : unam naturalem seu moralem, seu genus: altera pars est cæremonia, propria populo Israel, seu species de die septimo. De priore dicitur, naturale, seu genus esse perpetuu, & non posse abrogari : videlicet mandatu de conservado ministerio publico, sic ut aliquo die populus doceatur, & cæremoniæ divinitus institutæ exerceantur. Species vero, quæ nominatim de septimo die loquitur, abrogata est.

Ans. 1. Is he *Dolosus*, a deceiver, who maintaineth, there is a generall equitie in Divine Positive Lawes? No man living is able to justifie this. For in the Old Iudiciall Lawes, yea in many Ceremoniall Lawes, there is contained a generall Equity grounded upon the Law of Nature. In the *judiciall Law* set downe, *Exod.* 22. 1, 2. there is a generall equity implyed, obliging Christians to restitution of goods unjustly by them taken away. In the Law of *Deuteronomy* 25. 4.

Thou shalt not muzzle the mouth of the Oxe, that treadeth out the Corne, there was contained a generall naturall equity, 1 *Corinth.* 9. 9.

Therefore he is not *Dolosus*, who maintaineth a generall equity in the fourth Commandement, but he is *a Dolt who* denies it.

2 It is granted that the fourth Commandement is expresse for a certaine day, for a particular day: Namely for Saturday: *But* if it be expresse for Saturday, and for that Individuall day only, *Then* it is not expresse for *Sunday*: *and* the observation of *Sunday* must either be grounded upon the naturall equity of the fourth Commandement, *or* else it cannot be grounded upon that Commandement at all.

3 *Brother B.* saith in this passage of his Dialogue: *The* fourth Commandement is expresse for a certaine day: *But* in another of his treatises hee delivereth the contrary, to wit, *The Commandement saith not, Remember the Seventh day to sanctifie it: but Remember the Sabbath, whatsoever it be, to sanctifie it.* Now a certaine day, is *definite*: and a Sabbath day, whatsoever it be, is *indefinite*. Therefore if the fourth Commandement enjoyneth a Sabbath Day whatsoever it be, *it* commandeth a day indefinite, and not a particular and certaine day.

4 *If the fourth Commandement is expresse for the Lord's-Day, then it either nameth this day in particular, or it describeth the same by some Characters, by which it is distinguished from other dayes.*

But the Commandement neither nameth the Lord's

Lord's Day in particular, nor yet describeth it by any speciall Characters: *but* on the contrary it both nameth the Seventh day, and describeth it by a speciall Character, whereby it is distinguished from other dayes, *to wit*, by God's resting from his grand worke of prime Creation.

Therefore the fourth Commandement is not expresse for the keeping holy of the Lord's-day: but if wee will have the day expressely commanded, we must observe the Old Sabbath Day according to *Theoph. Brabourne's Tenet.*

5 Whereas the Objector saith: the Commandement must determine the particular time, and day *in Individuo*: because otherwise, if the same be left indetermined man should forget God, and himselfe, and allow no time at all for God's service:

The *answer is*, there can be no just reason, for people to forget God, and to allow no time at all for his service, *if* a sufficient and convenient time, be indefinitely commanded, by the Law of Nature, *and* a definite and particular day, and time be appointed by the Pastors of the Church. *For the precepts of the Church, being godly, and holy, and subservient to God's glory, and being grounded upon Apostolicall example, oblige Christian people to their particular duty, in observing time and place, and many other circumstances, concerning God's service: and* Christians are obliged to observe all such godly precepts, when the same are meanes to execute God's generall Law, which is: *Let all things in the Church be done decently, and in good order, and to edification*, &c. *pag. 99.*

B. It is a Law of nature, that every Lord and Master, should have the power in himselfe to appoint, not only the kinde of service, but the time when it should be performed of his servants : *As Alexander d. Ales* ᵃ saith upon the fourth Commandement. The time of this Rest, it is not in Man's power to determine, but God's.

<small>Alex. Hal. part. quæ 7. 32.</small>

Answ. The *chiefe Lord and Master of* the family hath the supreme authority, to determine the time, and circumstances of his owne service : *But* hee may delegate subordinate power to his *Steward*, or other Officers to performe the same.

In the Old Law, God Almighty prescribed the particular day, and place of his publike worship, to wit, the *Saturday* of every weeke, *&c.* and the *Tabernacle*, &c. *But* in the Evangelicall Law, he hath not expressely, or literally appointed either a particular day *or a particular place: But Christian Kings, being nursing Fathers,* and the Bishops, being Pastors and Governours in the Church, and *Stewards* of this great Lord, by a delegate and ministeriall power may lawfully performe this, *pag.* 187.

I desire the judicious Reader to consider, that the former Objection is *a pestilent drug, borrowed from Schismatickes and from Separatists,* pag. 95. and

and if the same bee admitted, it takes away all power from the Kings Majesty, and from the Church, to appoint *any set place* for God's publike service, or to ordaine any *holy dayes*, or festivall solemnities: or to determine the *houres of the day*, for peoples resorting to Church, and their continuance at the Church: Lastly, it denies the Churches power, of composing any *externall forme* or *Liturgy* for God's publike and solemne worship.

※※※※※※※※※※※※※※※

B. Againe, the Adversary acknowledgeth an equity in the fourth Commandement. What equity? If as it bound the ancient people of God, to one day in the weeke; it doe not also binde the Christian People to keep one day in the Weeke? And if it be the equity of the fourth Commandement, to prescribe one day in seven, then they are very unjust, that deny the keeping of the Lord's-Day, to be grounded upon the equity of the fourth Commandement.

It were well, if they would stand to equity: But this doth our Adversary flye from; for he saith in the next words: *The particular forme and circumstances of resting*

H 3   *are*

(54)

are *prescribed unto us by the precepts of the Church: our spirituall actions, according to that which is maine and substantiall in them, are taught by the Evangelicall Law. Their modification, and limitation in respect of rituall and externall forme: and in regard of place, duration, gesture, habit, and other externall circumstances, are prescribed by the Law of the Church.* So He.

Thus you see how hee limits the prescription of circumstances (which comprehend time and place, persons, and duration, when and how long God shall bee served) unto the prescription of the Law of the Church: which he expresseth more fully *pag.* 270. saying, *It was in the free election of the Church to appoint what day, or dayes or times she thought good, or found convenient for religious duties* [a] : For *the Evangelicall Law hath not determined any certain day or time:* And those actions, or circumstances, which are not determined by divine precept, are permitted to the liberty and authority of the Church, to be determined and appointed. So *He.*

But cleare it is, that the Church of England

[a] P. Martyr *in Genes.* 2. Quod hic dies magis quam ille eligatur ad Dei cultum, liberū fuit ecclesiæ per Christum, ut id consuleret, quod magis ex re judicaret. Bulling. *Cō. in Apoc.* 1. 10. Sponte vero Ecclesiæ recepta cum illam diem, non legimus eam alibi præceptam. Hospin. *de Orig. Fest. ca.* 8. Et si ex his constet Dominicum diem jam tum Apostolorum temporibus Judaici Sabbathi loco fuisse solennem, non inveniuntur tamen vel Apostolos, vel alios lege aliqua aut præcepto observationi ejus instituisse, sed illam fuisse liberam, &c. In primitiva Ecclesia ipsius quoq; Dominicæ diei observatio nulla certa lege recepta, sed libera fuit, &c.

land disclaimeth all such power [a] : but ascribes all authority, of prescribing a time and day of holy rest, unto the *Lord* of the Sabbath, who hath expressed his will and pleasure herein, in his Law of the fourth Commandement, as our Homily saith.

[a] *Reade the words of the Statute, recited in the Preface to the Reader: and it will be evident that Br. B. is a deceiver.*

Answ. The *Bishop* acknowledgeth a morall equity in the fourth Commandement, for the observation of *necessary, sufficient and convenient times, dayes, houres,* &c. *For Gods publike worship, and the performance of spirituall and Religious offices.* And (for ought this Objector hath said or can say to the contrary) more than this, cannot bee proved out of the Law of the fourth Commandement, *or by* any necessary illation, from any sentence of the Commandement; *Or* from any principle of the Law of Nature [b].

For the Principle of naturall Law is: *God is duly and religiously to be worshipped:* but unlesse convenient, and sufficient time be appointed, God Almighty cannot bee duly and religiously worshipped, *Therefore* a necessary, convenient, and sufficient time, must bee appointed [c] (either expressely by God Himselfe, or by such as he hath ordained to bee his *Stewards,* and Officers in the Church) for Divine worship.

2 The fourth Commandement enjoyned the *Iewes* to keepe holy the seventh day, being our Saturday: but from hence we cannot conclude by necessary inference, that the fourth Commandement enjoyneth Christians to keep holy the Sunday

[b] *Lorca. 1. 2. de leg. Disp. 8. Legis naturæ alia sunt prima principia practica, per se nota: alia sunt conclusiones ex principiis deductæ, conclusiones autem aliæ universaliores, & proximiores primis principiis: aliæ quæ a primis principiis, magis distant, & sunt specialiores, & de particularibus objectis.*

[c] *Alex Hal. 3 7. 33 m. 1. De ratione bene ordinati est, quod cum semper non possimus vacare Deo, propter temporales, & corporales necessitates, quod aliquando vacemus: oportet igitur habere tempus aliquod determinatum.*

Sunday being the first day of the weeke: *For the speciall and proper materiall object of every Law, is a substantiall part of that Law*; but if the substantiall part of any Law be changed and taken away, *a new Subject or materiall Object is no part of the old Law*; *but another law must be ordained*, for the setling of that new Subject, and materiall object in the place of the former.

3 Whereas the Objector pretendeth, that the Church of *England* disclaimeth all power of setling the particular time of God's publike worship; *how* then commeth it to passe, that this Church commandeth the solemne observation of *Easter*, *Whitsuntide*, *Christmasse*, and of many other Holy-dayes, to be dayes and times for the religious service of God and Christ.

꙳꙳꙳꙳꙳꙳꙳꙳꙳꙳꙳꙳꙳

A. But the Homily seemes to favour his opinion, saying, *godly* Christian people began to chuse them a standing day of the weeke, &c. and therefore it seemes to be at the Churches choyce.

B. Our choyce doth not necessarily imply a power of institution; *we are* said to chuse life and truth, before death and error, *are we* therefore the Authors of them? *Againe*, our choyce herein is according to God's Commandement.

Thirdly,

(57)

Thirdly, the Homily saith expressely, that those godly Christian people, did in their choyce follow the example and Commandement of God. Now what example ᶜ had they but Christ's rising, and resting that day after the example of God's resting the seventh day. And for Commandement, they had both the fourth Commandement, and an Apostolicall Precept, 1 *Cor.* 16. ᵈ And that place in the *Revelation* appropriating this Day, as holy to the Lord, and so ratified by God himselfe: And who were they which taught those godly Christian people to keep that day ? *viz.* The Apostles.

And therefore we must put a vast difference betweene the unerring Apostles, and the succeeding Churches, so as the Homily is cleare against him.

Answ. The Objector saith: *The Churches choice doth not necessarily imply a power of institution, &c.*

It is answered: making choyce many times implyes a free election, and institution, both in Scripture, *Deut.* 26. 2. 1 *Sam* 17. 8. and in Ecclesiasticall and Humane Authors: and that it is thus to be understood in the Homily, is proved in manner following :

The sense of the Homily is according to the authorized Doctrine of the Church of *England*.

I   But

ᶜ The *Example of God*, specified in the fourth Commandement ; was his own resting & ceasing upon the olde Sabbath Day, from the worke of prime Creation and not our Saviour his resting from the work of Resurrection, upon the first day of the weeke.

ᵈ No generall commandement common to all Christians, for the weekely observation of Sunday, is delivered in these two Texts of holy Scripture.

But the authorized Doctrine of the Church of *England* is, *That the appointment both of the time and number of dayes, is left by the authority of Gods Word to the liberty of the Church, to be assigned orderly by the discretion of the Rulers and Ministers thereof, as they shall judge most expedient to the true setting forth of Gods glory, and the edification of the people.*

Ergo, the Churches choyce, according to the Homily, is a free election of a convenient day, and of other convenient and sufficient time, for the service of God, and the edification of Christian people.

2 There is *a great difference betweene a Precept and an Example.* The Homily saith, that godly Christians (to wit, *by imitation of God's example*) observed a seventh day; but it affirmeth not, that they did this by an expresse Commandement of any Divine Law.

Also godly *Christians made the fourth Commandement of the Decalogue a motive to induce them,* to make one day of seven a weekly Holy day; but *that which is only a motive, or a reason inducing* and perswading to performe an action, *is not an expresse, imperative, or formall Law.*

The sense therefore of the Homily is, *That Christians made choyce of a weekely standing day by the rule of the equity of the fourth Commandement, and not by any expresse or formall Divine Law* c.

Nec Causa d Sab. Nec Christus, nec ipsi Apostoli ex quarto to Christi, de observatione hujus diei ulla expressim indicaverunt, quemadmodum de aliis pietatis officiis reliquerunt. Non videtur autem ullo modo verisimile, ut Christus vel ad observationem illius diei, ut partem cultus voluisset astringere, fuisse factum, nisi nullo praecepto indicasset. Bulling. *Apoc 2. Non legimus eam ulli bi praeceptam.* Hospinian *d sed. cap 8. Non invenitur Apostolos aut alios lege aliqua aut praecepto observationem ejus instituisse.*

3 Our

3 Our Saviour's Resurrection upon one Sunday in the yeare, cannot of it selfe, unlesse some precept were added, be a Law to enjoyne Christians to observe every Sunday of the Weeke throughout the whole yeare; read. *pag.* 302.

4 The fourth Commandement is directly and in plaine termes for Saturday, *pag.* 182, 183. *and* therefore if that Commandement is still in force according to the literall sense, then the Christian Church is obliged to observe the old legall Sabbath; for the Objector hath formerly rejected the equity of the fourth Commandement, and therefore he must wholly ground his Tenet upon the expresse words, or upon some necessary and formall illation from the words or sentences of that Commandement.

5 In S. *Pauls* Text, 1 *Cor.* 16. 2. we find a mandate, that the *Corinthians* upon the first day of the weeke should lay aside something for charitable uses, according as God had enabled them; and more than this we reade not in that Text.

6 The Place, *Revel.* 1. 10. containes no mandate; for no imperative words are found therein, but only a narration of the time, in which S. *Iohn* received his Propheticall Revelation.

Lastly, the Bishop is perswaded, that the holy Apostles (not presently, or immediately, but) certaine yeares after Christ's Resurrection, taught Christian people to observe the Lord's-day, 109. 189. *But* this impetuous Objector cannot demonstrate, that the holy Apostles themselves, or their immediate Successours, grounded the observation of this day upon the old Law of the 4th Commandement.

And therefore we trust *Br. B.* will not take it unkindely that we cannot yeeld assent to his verball Positions, which are not confirmed by Divine or Ecclesiasticall testimony, nor yet by any other weighty grounds of reason; and lastly they are repugnant to the common Tenet of the most judicious Divines ancient and moderne.

❦❦❦❦❦❦❦❦❦❦❦❦❦❦❦ ❦❦❦❦❦❦❦❦❦❦❦❦❦❦❦

A. The maine knot of the whole Controversie, is about the designation of the particular and speciall time consecrated to Gods worship: whether it be comprehended and prescribed in the fourth Commandement, or depends upon the determination of the Church.

The Adversary confesseth a naturall equity in the fourth Commandement; That some time is to be set apart for the service of God, but indeputate, and left at large to the liberty of the Church, to determine and limit the speciall time, when and how long, what portion, and proportion is to be allowed, &c. I pray you more fully elucidate this Point, &c.

Ans. 1. The Bishop's Tenet is, *That by the equity naturall of the fourth Commandement, a necessary sufficient,*

sufficient, and convenient time ought to bee appointed by the Christian Church, for Divine worship, and for religious offices. Therefore it is not left to the Churches liberty and arbitterment, to allow what portion or proportion of time it pleaseth; *For it must in duty and obedience to God, proportion a full, convenient, and sufficient time.*

2 The Church shall doe that which is offensive, if without just, necessary, and urgent cause, it presume to remove the ancient bounds, or to alter the ordinance of primitive times, concerning the religious observance of the Lord's-day. For the Tradition [a] of the Holy Apostles, and of the Primitive and Apostolicall Church, ought highly to be honoured and respected: *and* (according to Saint *Augustines* [b] rule) *it is insolent madnesse* (unlesse it be done upon necessary reason) to vary from the same, *pag.* 270.

[a] Hieron. *Dial. feq. Pelagian. Scripturæ authoritas non subsistit, totius orbis in hanc partem consensus instar præcepti obtinet. Ni & multa alia, quæ per Traditionem in Ecclesiis observantur, authoritatem sibi scriptæ legis usurpaverunt.*
[b] Aug. *Ep. 118 ad Januar. cap. 5.*

✤✤✤✤✤✤✤✤✤✤✤✤✤✤✤✤✤✤✤✤✤✤✤✤✤✤✤

B. The Adversary doth the more *easily play fast and loose* [c] in the myst of his generalities, *though* while hee cannot or dare not for shame utterly deny the morality of the fourth Commandement (which all Divines doe hold:) *yet* he denies any particular, speciall, determinate time to be commanded, or limited therein, but will have

[c] *Observe, how this bould B. asserteth, and in the end falseth in his proofe.*

I 3

that

that wholly put and placed in the power of the Church.

It will be requisite therefore *to stop this hole* [a], that he may not have the least evasion, but by *the cords of strong reasons* [b] be bound and forced to confesse, *That* either the fourth Commandement doth prescribe and determine a set, certaine, fixed proportion of time, consecrated by God himselfe unto his solemne and sacred worship: *Or else that it commands to Vs Christians no certaine time or day at all : and so the morality of it (if ever it had any) is quite abolished, and no other Law or Commandement now binds us, but the precept or practise of the Church. This* is the very Summe and upshot of the matter.

You will stop this hole, with bold prating onely.
b. Your cordes of strong reason, will prove ropes of sand and cordes of vanitie.

Answ. 1. The Bishop delivered all his Positions, and Assertions, concerning the Sabbath, in perspicuous, distinct, and clear Sentences, Termes, and Propositions, in which there is no ambiguity, no equivocation, no fast and loose, as this *Boldface* declameth.

2 He hath confirmed the said Positions, with strong and weighty reasons (the most of them are Demonstrative:) and his Arguments are such, as this Objector is afraid to looke upon them: *and* throughout his Dialogue, like unto a *Cravin Cur*, he

he bites behinde, at the conclusion, but dares not looke the Premises of the Arguments in the face.

3 *It was not feare or shame* that induced the Bishop to maintain the naturall equity of the fourth Commandement, *but love of verity, and weight of reason, and the consent of grave and judicious Divines: But* neither *feare nor shame* can perswade this *rude animall* [a], who is *maledicus conviciator, non veridicus Disputator*, to deliver any thing materiall, or which favoureth of common reason.

[a] *Homine imperito nihil est improbius. Qui nisi quod ipse facit nihil rectù putat.*

4 The Position, that the morality of the fourth Commandement must be utterly abolished, unlesse it command us Christians a definite and particular day, as it did the *Iewes*, is an idle and presumptuous position, as will appeare by the loose and inepte Arguments which the *Dialogaster* brings to confirme the same.

✼✼✼✼✼✼✼✼✼✼✼✼✼✼✼✼✼✼

B. Now I shall prove and make it evident, that the fourth Commandement either prescribes a certaine proportion of time, and *a fixed day* [b], consecrate to God, and in that very respect is perpetually morall, binding us Christians to the same proportion: *or else* if it determine no set proportion of time, but *leaves it at large* [c] to the *Church* to proportionate, whether longer or shorter: *Then* there remaines no such
obligatory

[b] *The fourth Commandement appointed a particular fixed day, to wit, Saturday; and if it is in that very respect morall, why doth H. B. condemne Th. Brab. if it serves it not at large, but the equity and analoge of the Commandement obligeth the church to appoint certaine convenient and sufficient time.*

obligatory equity in the fourth Commandement, as to binde the Church to appoint and allow such or such a proportion of time: *but that if this time which the Church appointeth, be either one day in twenty, or forty, or an hundred, or one day in the yeere, or so; or but one piece of a day in such a revolution of time, and not one whole or intire day, much lesse one whole day in every seven: The Church in this sinneth not, as being not guilty of the breach of the fourth Commandement, which bindeth us Christians to no certaine proportion of time, as the Adversary himselfe would have it, but in this respect is now abrogated,* &c.

Answ. The Objector at his entrance saith: *Now I shall prove and make it evident*, &c. and then falsifieth his word, for his Argument is of no force at all.

If (saith Br. B.) *the naturall equity of the fourth Commandement determineth not one particular and certaine day of the week, but only a sufficient and convenient time for Divine worship:* Then *there is no obligatory equity in the fourth Commandement. And the Church sinneth not, if it appoint one day in twenty, forty, a hundred, or one day, or halfe a day in a yeere, or in an age,* &c.

But

But the Adversary maintaineth, that the naturall equity of the fourth Commandement prescribeth only a sufficient and convenient time, but no one certaine or fixed day of the weeke. Ergo.

The Adversary leaveth it in the Churches liberty, and arbiterment to allow as small a proportion of time, to wit, one day in 20. 40. 100. *or in the whole yeare, &c. as it pleaseth.*

The consequence of the former argument is a Lame Giles; for one day in 20. 40. 100. or in the whole yeare, *Or one halfe day in a Weeke, Moneth, or Yeare, &c.* is not a competent and sufficient time for God's service, or for religious duties, and for the spirituall edification of Christian people: *Therefore* the naturall equity of *the fourth Commandement, requiring a necessary competent and sufficient time for Divine worship,* obligeth the Church to allow a greater measure, and proportion of time, than one only day in 20. 40. 100. *&c.*

B. Argument 1. Observe we the words of the Commandement, Remember the Sabbath Day [a] to keepe it holy: which words (saith the learned *Zanchy* [b]) are the very morall substance of the fourth Commandement. *The* Lord saith not, remember to sanctifie some convenient, and sufficient time, as the Church shall thinke fit:

K

[a] Præmittitur memento, quia nimirum, cum non sit naturale præceptũ poterant illud facile Iudæi oblivisci.
[b] Zanc. d. oper. Redemp. in 4. Mand. Adjecimus, sine ulla conscientiæ obligatione, fuisse hunc diem divino cultui destinatum. Hoc liquet è sacris literis. Nullibi enim legimus Apostolos hoc cuipiam mandasse: tantum legimus quid soliti fuerint facere Apostoli & fideles illo die: liberum igitur reliquerunt. Waleus de Sabb. pag. 156. Nec Christus nec ipsi Apost. ex præscripto Christi de observatione hujus diei, ullum expressum mandatum, quemadmodum de aliis pietatis officiis reliquerunt.

The

The Commandement prescribeth a certaine and set time, yea a day, the Sabbath Day, one day in the weeke, which is the Sabbath day.

Againe, it teacheth what day in the week the Sabbath day is: to wit, the Sabbath day of the Lord thy God: *that day* in the weeke wherein the Lord our God resteth, must bee our Sabbath Day. So that as the Commandement prescribes unto us a weekely Sabbath day to be sanctified; So God's president and example points out unto Vs, what or which day in the weeke we must rest on, to sanctifie it. *And* this is not only the naturall equity (which the Adversary in generall confesseth) but the very naturall Law, and substance of the fourth Commandement, to prescribe a set solemne day in the weeke to be sanctified, and not to leave it in the power of Man, or of the Church, to appoint what time they please:

The Reasons are these: 1. *because* the Commandement expressely limiteth one set day in the week, being the Sabbath day of the Lord our God. *Now* the Commandement

ment prescribing a set and fixed day in the weeke, what humane power shall dare to alter it into an indefinite time (call it what you will, convenient or sufficient) to be appointed at the pleasure of man? *This is* with the Papists to commit high sacriledge, in altering the property of God's Commandements. *For* upon this ground of generall equity, they have beene bold to suppresse the second Commandement, saying it is comprised in the first. *As* they have robbed the people of the Cup in the Sacrament, saying the bloud is contained in the body under the formes of Bread. *So our Adversary* imagining a generall (I wot not what) equity in the fourth Commandement of some certaine uncertaine time, for God's publike worship, doth thereby destroy the very propertie of the Commandement, which **expressely** prescribeth the Sabbath Day in every weeke.

Answ. 1. This argument is downe right for *Theophilus Brabourne's* Tenet, concerning the Saturday Sabbath; *For* Saturday is the set, fixed and particular day in the weeke, concerning which God said, *Remember the Sabbath day to keep it holy.* That *speciall weekely day, which is called the*

Sabbath of the Lord thy God: This only day, and no other, was it, *In* which the Lord God rested from the worke of prime Creation: *and* God's example expressed in the fourth Commandement, pointed out this particular day of the weeke, and not any other of the sixe dayes. The Law and substance of the fourth Commandement, was fulfilled in the religious observation of this very day, *and* during the time of the Old Law, it was not in the power of the Church, or of any humane creature to alter this day into any other.

Now from hence it is consequent, that if the Christian Church stands obliged to observe that weekely day, *which was stiled the Sabbath of the Lord thy God,* and which is thus marked, and pointed out in the fourth Commandement; *Then* wee must observe the Legall Sabbath day according to *Th. Brab.* his Tenet.

It might bee admired (but that *the pride and stupid ignorance of this Goose-quill is notorious*) that he should not foresee the consequence so directly concluding for the observation of the Old Legall Sabbath.

Secondly, Whereas this *Babler* saith, that they which deny, that the fourth Commindement, in time of the Gospell, prescribeth a set and fixed weekely day for publike worship, comply with the Papists, who take away the second Commandement, and the Cup from the people, &c.

Our answer is. 1. *Let* him resolve us, whether *Calvin, Beza, Bullinger, P. Martir, Rivetus* [b], &c. who maintained the former position, complied with the Papists.

[b] Rivet. *in Exod.* 20. *pag* 184. Quæstio agitatur, in saltem unus è septem diebus, etsi non à creatione septimus, sed in unaquaq; septimana, in orbe recurrés septimus, ex quarti præcepti vi, ut qua morale est, sit necessario observandus in Ecclesia Christiana. Resp. *pag.* 186. Argumenta pro negativa parte illa sunt, ut me moveant ne discedam ab ea quam Calvinus probavit sententia.

2 He

2 Hee should first have proved by firme arguments (*but his manner is to prate, and not to prove,*) that Christians, under the Gospell, have received an expresse Commandement from *God*, for the Observation of a certaine particular day in every weeke ; *In* such manner, as they have received the Commandements, touching the nor-adoration of Images, and giving the Cup in the Eucharist. *But* untill hee performe this (which will bee impossible) hee declareth himselfe a Rude Accuser: and withall a foolish, and babling disputer.

✼✼✼✼✼✼✼✼✼✼✼✼✼✼✼✼✼✼✼✼✼✼

B. A second reason, why it is not left in the power of the Church to Prescribe what time men please, is : *Because* it is God's prerogative as a Master, to appoint his owne worship, and service ; *So the time* a *wherein hee will bee served.* This God *Himselfe commandeth in the fourth Commandement.* Now as the King will not take it well, that any meddle with his prerogative, and arrogate that to himselfe, which is the King's right : *So God is justly offended, when men presume to assume to themselves that power, which is proper, and peculiar to God alone* b.

a *The time commanded in the fourth Commandement is Saturday, the Old Legall Sabbath.*

b *God is wel pleased when the Church assumeth such ministeriall power, as he hath granted.*

If any will take upon him to coine money by counterfeiting the King's stamp and name, his act is Treason. *How* then shall they escape, who presume to coine what time they please for God's solemne worship, though they set the counterfeit stamp of God upon it. *Now the Sabbath Day is of the Lord's owne making c and stamping, and therefore called the Lord's Day.*

a The Sabbath day of the fourth Commandement was of God's owne immediate making: and if this day, is the Lord's day, Then Th. Br. is a little right.

Answ. There is no colour of truth in this second reason.

1 The Author of it dealeth falsely: For *the Bishop maintaineth not, that it is in the Churches power to appoint what time men please for Divine Worship*: But hee saith the contrary, to wit, *The Church must appoint such a measure and proportion of time for God's worship, and for Religious Offices, as is convenient, competent, and every way sufficient*: But hee that teacheth this, leaveth it not in the power and liberty of the Church to prescribe what time men please: *Because* such time as men please to appoint, may be inconvenient, incompetent, and insufficient, for so great and holy a worke.

2 The argument it selfe is of no force: For although all power of constituting time, for his owne worship, bee *eminently and originally* in God himselfe, as likewise is the teaching of all supernaturall truth, *Matth.* 23. 8. *Yet* there is given to the Pastors of the Church, *a derivative*

delegate

delegate, and ministeriall power, both to teach God's people, and likewise to appoint set, fixed, and convenient dayes, and times and places, for religious worship, *pag.* 187.

Where the great Lord and Master himselfe hath by his owne expresse, or immediate Law, ordained a particular day or time, for his owne worship, *It* is not lawfull for man, to alter the same: *and* therefore the Iewes in the Old Law, might not change their Sabbath into another day: *But the Church by ministeriall, and delegate power, may adde, and increase the number of Religious holy dayes,* if it be necessary or expedient for the peoples edification.

For in the very time of the Old Law, when many festivall dayes were ordained by God's speciall mandate, *the* Iewish Church, notwithstanding, upon speciall occasions, appointed some new Holy Dayes, *Hest.* 9. 17. 1 *Machab.* 4. 56. *and our blessed Saviour Himselfe* honoured one of these feasts, with his owne presence, *Ioh.* 10. 22. *But* now in the time of the N. Test. the Church of Christ must of necessity have power, to ordain set times, and festivall dayes, for Divine worship, and the spirituall edification of People; *because* such dayes and times are necessary to the ends aforesaid: *and* the Lord Himselfe by no expresse particular mandate of Holy Scripture hath commanded them.

3 The Objector's similitudes borrowed from Royall Prerogative, and coining or stamping monies, are nothing worth: for although no Subject may lawfully usurpe the Kings's authority

or

or prerogative: *yet a Subject may receive power from the King's authority and Prerogative, to do many things, which otherwise were unlawfull for him to doe: As* appeareth in *Iudges,* who from the King's prerogative in sundry cases have power of life and death: *In privy Counsellors, &c.* So likewise the Pastors of the Christian Church, by *a Ministeriall power,* given them by Christ, exercise authority many wayes in ordering times and places, and many other actions, and circumstances which concerne God's worship.

Also it is very lawfull for subjects to Coine and stampe monies, when the King being supreme Lord, granteth them licence and authority: *It is* Treason in such only, as presume to doe it without license: *and* because it is a thing prohibited by Lawes and Royall Authority. *And* so it fareth with the Governours, in the Christian Church: *If* they presume to appoint any thing, which God hath prohibited, they are Delinquents: *But* if in their Ecclesiasticall Precepts they exceed not the power given them by Christ they doe well, and they ought to be obeyed.

4. This *Mangie Objection* (which the Dialogue dropper hugs in his bosome, and when *he blatters it out of his wooden deske,* he is applauded with the *loud Hem* of his seduced Auditory) is borrowed from Old *Thomas Cartwright,* who, in his dayes poysoned many credulous people with such *Scabby Similitudes,* and with some other such like popular insinuations, *pag. 95.*

B.

B. A third Reason, why it is not left in Man's power to institute the solemne day of God's worship, his Sabbath Day, or to appoint him what proportion of time they please, is : *Because* an indefinite time must either binde to all moments of time, as a debt, when the day of payment is not expressely dated, is liable to payment every moment : *Or else* it bindes to no time at all [a].

For if the Law of God binde Vs not to an expresse, determinate time or day consecrate to his service : *Then the not allowing of him a set time or day, is no sin at all. For what God's Law commands not, therein man is not bound : And where no set Law is of a set time or day, there is no transgression, if a set time or day be not observed.* So as by this reason, If the Law of the 4th. Commandement prescribe no set sacred time or day for rest and sanctification, it is a meere Nullity. For to say there is a naturall equity in it for some sufficient and convenient

[a] The naturall equity of God's positive Law, requires convenient, and sufficient time. The precept of the Church determines the day or time in speciall. Now that being performed, the day and time for the solemne worship of God, is made definite and certaine.

nient time, *and yet no man can define, what this sufficient and convenient time is; nay all* the heads and wits in the world put together, are not able to determine it, *it is as to* say, there is a world in the Moone, consisting of Land and Sea, and inhabitants, because there are some blacke spots in it: which is yet *not a more Lunaticke opinion*, than that is presumptuous and absurd.

Hath not the profane world found by woefull experience, and that of late dayes, within these two yeares last past, wherein men have taken a liberty to prophane and pollute but a part of the Lord's Day, that this is a most horrible sin? *And* a sin it cannot be, but as a breach of one of God's Holy Commandements; *for* where there is no Law, there is no transgression. *The* profanation (I say) of the Lord's Day is clearely shewed to bee an horrible presumptuous sin, and in speciall *a bold breach* of the fourth Commandement, by those many remarkeable judgements of God, which have fearefully fallen upon feareleſſe Sabbath breakers, and that (I say)
within

within thefe two yeares laft paft, the like whereof cannot be parallell'd in all the Hiſtories of all the *Centuries* fince the Apoſtles times.

Which alone (if men were not altogether poſſeſſed with the ſpirit of ſtupidity, and of a croced conſcience) were ſufficient to teach their dull wits, that the fourth Commandement is ſtill in force, commanding the Sabbath-day to be ſanctified, the profanation whereof we ſee ſo terribly puniſhed by divine revenge. A point alſo which our Homily hath noted: *which were ſufficient to admoniſh the Adverſary of his preſumptuous oppoſitions thereunto.*

Anſw. 1. Divine Lawes being generall, or indefinite, oblige to obedience in particulars, *when the ſpeciall Object commanded or prohibited by any other juſt Lawes, is reduced to the Divine generall Law by lawfull conſequence.* For example: *Thou ſhalt not ſteale*, is generall: *Therefore thou ſhalt not without licenſe from the Owner, or without other lawfull authority, take away thy Neighbours Oxe or his Aſſe: and yet Meum and Tuum,* thy Neighbours Oxe and his Aſſe, are made his owne by humane Law. *So likewiſe in* is preſent Queſtion, *the generall equity of the*

L 2 *Divine*

Divine Law, is; *Christian* people must observe a convenient and sufficient time for Divine Worship, &c. *And* Christian Princes, and the Bishops and Pastors of the Church, having lawfull Authority to appoint such Observations as are subservient to true Religion, have ordained *Christmasse, Easter,* and the *Lord's-day* of every Weeke for Divine Worship and Religious Duties: *Ergo,* Christians are obliged by the generall Equity of the Divine Law, to observe *Christmasse, Easter,* and the *Lord's-day,* after that the Rulers and Pastors of the Church have appointed the same to be done to God's glory.

It is *a frantick Paradox* to maintaine, That Christians are obliged to nothing, but such things only as are definitely and in particular commanded, by some expresse written Law of GOD in holy Scripture: *For* many things which are in Nature and kinde indifferent, when they are commanded by *Parents, Masters, Magistrates,* or any other lawfull authority, come within the compasse of God's generall Law, and that generall Law obligeth people to performe them; *Mediante Præcepto Parentis, Heri, Magistratus, Ecclesiæ, &c.* by a mediate precept of Parent, Master, Magistrate, or Church, *pag.* 93.

2 To the Objector's Argument, the answer is; *Where* God's Law commandeth not, either in particular or in generall, there is no sin: *but if* God's Law command in generall, *That we must obey every lawfull ordinance of the Church, being subservient to God's glory, and the edification of his people: and* the Church commandeth us religiously

to

to observe the Lord's-day; *Christian* people are bound in conscience to obey [a]: *and if they doe otherwise, they transgresse God's Commandement, and are guilty of sin, pag. 93.*

3 Whereas this *Scribler* affirmeth, *that no man is able to define a convenient and sufficient time for God's worship, &c. and* compares the undertaking thereof to the imagination of the being of *a World in the Moone, &c.* I doubt not but that this quaint conceit, makes him *prick up his eares: but* upon due examination it will prove as ridiculous as *the Man in the Moone: For* if any one presume to define things which are remote from humane cognisance, not having sufficient meanes to prove his affirmation, *he* justly deserves to be condemned of rashnesse and folly: *But* the Governours in the Christian Church, want not compleat and sufficient meanes to enable them to set downe and determine, convenient and sufficient time for God's publike worship: *for* they have many *generall Rules*, laid downe in holy Scripture, for the ordering of Ecclesiasticall affaires: *they* have likewise *Presidents of the Divine Law* in ancient time: *they* have *the practise and example* of the Saints of God to direct and leade them: *and Christian prudence* hath enabled them in former ages to appoint sufficient and convenient dayes and times for God's solemne worship: *and* in these dayes, they have both understanding, and authority to do the like.

4 God's vengeance upon malicious profaners of the Lord's-day, is no sufficient argument to prove, that this day is expressely or literally commanded

[a] Bernard. *d. præcept. & Dispens. cap 12.* Sive Deus, sive homo vicarius Dei mandatum quodcunq, tradiderit, pari profecto obsequendum est cura, pari reverentia deferendum, ubi tamen Deo contraria non præcepit homo

commanded, to be observed in the Christian Church, by the particular Precept of the fourth Commandment. For wilfull transgression of the Precepts of the Church, commanding such actions and others, as are religious, holy, and subservient to God's glory, brings God's heavie judgements upon profane and disobedient people.

S In the close of the former Argument, *Brother B.* casts dirt in the Face of him whom he stileth his Adversary; saying, *This were sufficient to admonish the Adversary of his presumptuous oppositions thereunto.* But where, or when, hath his Adversary delivered any Position in his late Treatise, or elsewhere, in defence *of profaneness* upon the Lord's day, or upon any other day? For honest and sober recreation upon some part of the Holyday, *is farre more remote from profaneness, than the factious and viperous deportments of this Roarer,* against such as comply not with him in his presumptuous Dictats.

B. Mr. *Hooker, Ecclef. Pol. lib.* 5. Sect 70. hath these words: *If it be demanded whether we observe these times* (to wit, Holy-dayes) *as being thereunto bound by force of Divine Law, or else by the only positive Ordinances of the Church: I answer to this, That the very Law of Nature*

it

it felfe, which all Men confeffe to be God's Law, requireth *in generall*, no leffe the fanctification of times, than of places, perfons, and things unto God's honour. For which caufe it hath pleafed him heretofore, as of the reft, fo of time likewife to exact fome parts by way of perpetuall homage, never to be difpenfed withall, nor remitted: againe, to require fome other parts of time with as ftrict exaction, but for leffe continuance; and of the reft which were leffe arbitrary, to accept what the Church fhall in due confideration confecrate voluntarily unto like religious ufes.

Of the firft kind, among the *Iewes*, was the Sabbath-day: *Of* the fecond, thofe Feafts which are appointed in the Law of *Mofes*. *The* Feaft of Dedication, invented by the Church, ftandeth in the number of the laft kind. *The* Morall Law requiring therefore a feventh part throughout the age of the whole world to be that way imployed, although with Vs the day be changed, in regard of a new revolution begun by our *Saviour Chrift* : yet the fame proportion of time continueth which was before;

fore; because in reference to the benefit of Creation, and now much more of Renovation thereunto added by Him, which was Prince of the World to come; we are bound to account the sanctification of one day in seven, a duty which God's immutable Law doth exact for ever.

You see that in termes he agreeth, and jumpeth with the expresse Doctrine of our Church, in the Homily touching the perpetuall morality of the fourth Commandement: *We are bound* (saith he) *to account the sanctification of one day in seven,* (which before he saith is now our Lord's-day) *a duty which God's immutable Law doth exact for ever.*

Answ. Mr. H. in the passage aforesaid, delivereth nothing in substance differing from the Bishop.

1 He saith, that God's naturall Law requireth the sanctification of times in generall: and he affirmeth the same concerning *places, persons*[a]*, &c.* But the sanctification of *particular places*, is required by no expresse speciall Law in the new Testament, but onely by the equity or generall Law of Nature, and the practise and example of holy people in ancient times.

2 He affirmeth not, that the observation of the

the Lord's-day is commanded by speciall and expresse words of the fourth Commandement, for he acknowledgeth *a generall Law only*, which can be no other but *the naturall Equity and Analogie* of the fourth Commandement.

✦✦✦✦✦✦✦✦✦✦✦✦✦✦✦ ✦✦✦✦✦✦✦✦✦✦✦✦✦✦

B. Bishop *Andrewes* saith, &c. It hath ever beene the Churches Doctrine, that Christ made an end of all Sabbaths by his Sabbath in the Grave: *That* Sabbath was the last of them. *And* that the Lord's-day presently came in place of it.

The Lord's-day was by the Resurrection of Christ declared to be the Christians day: and from that very time (of Christ's Resurrection) it began to be celebrated as the Christian Man's Festivall. *For* the Sabbath had reference to the old Creation, but in Christ we are a new Creature, a new Creation by him, and to have a new Sabbath, &c.

Answ. 1. If *Christ* (according to Bishop *Andrewes*) *made an end of all Sabbaths*, then he made an end of the Sabbath of the fourth Commandement. *And* from hence it is consequent, that the Sabbath of the fourth Commandement was
not

not simply morall, or of the Law of Nature; for that which is such, is unchangeable and perpetuall: *and* besides, the observation of the Lord's-day, cannot be enjoyned by a Law or Commandement which is ceased.

2 Bp. *Andrewes* saying, *The* Lord's-day was declared to be the Christians festivall by the *Resurrection of Christ*, and was celebrated rather than any other Day, proveth, that the celebration thereof, was not grounded upon the speciall Law of the fourth Commandement (as this Dialogist hath formerly said) but upon our Saviour's Resurrection. *Neither* doth the *learned Bishop* teach, that it was grounded upon *Christ's Resurrection* as upon a Law: *but* according to the common vote of all Antiquity, his meaning must be, that *our Saviour's Resurrection was a motive* perswading and inducing the Christian Church to observe that day rather than any other.

Lastly, by new Sabbath, the Bishop understandeth the *Christian Sabbatisme*, which is, ceasing and resting from the deeds of sin, especially upon *the Lord's-day*, and upon other Festivall dayes which are devoted to godlinesse, and to Religious Offices.

✠✠✠✠✠✠✠✠✠✠✠✠✠✠✠✠✠✠✠✠✠✠✠✠

B. Bp. *Andrewes* in a Catecheticall Tractate delivereth these following: That the old Sabbath was no Ceremony. The day is changed, but no Ceremony proved.

It

It were not wise to set a Ceremony in the midd'st of morall Precepts. The Law of Nature is the Image of GOD: Now in GOD there can be no Ceremony, &c. The Law of the Decalogue is totally of the Law of Nature.

Now from the Premises we observe, what was the judgement of that *learned Prelate*, &c. *He* sheweth plainly, that the Lord's-day comming in place of the old Sabbath-day, and so becomming our Sabbath-day, is by necessary consequence grounded upon the fourth Commandement, the Law whereof is perpetuall, because naturally morall. So as hence I might frame this Argument: *That day which comes in place of the old Sabbath, is commanded in the fourth Commandement*: But the Lord's-day is come in place of the old Sabbath: *Therefore* it is commanded in the fourth Commandement.

Answ. 1. It is not certaine to Vs, that *Bishop Andrewes* was the Author of the *Patterne of Catecheticall Doctrine*, cited by the Objector: or if in his younger daies, before hee had throughly examined the Question of the *Sabbath*, he delivered the passage here mentioned, yet after his riper yeares, and when hee was come to maturity of judgement, he hath not in any Tractate, published by himselfe, while he was living, or by *some Reverend Bishops*, after his decease, maintained the former Doctrine.

And in very deed, hee could not, in his riper yeares (*being a man of great learning, and judgement, and throughly versed in Antiquity*) maintaine the same.

For 1. *It is apparently false, and repugnant to Scripture, and all Antiquitie, that the fourth Commandement was intirely morall, and had no Ceremony in it. This is effectually proved* by the Bishop, page 161. 163. &c. and all exceptions and objections to the contrary, are solved and cleared.

2 It is an infallible Verity, that the Law of the fourth Commandement, in respect of one determinate weekely day, was temporary, and legally positive ª. Read the *Bishop's* Treatise, pag. 28. 29. 30. &c.

3 *Bishop Andrewes* having said, The Lord's-Day presently came in place of the Old Sab. *The rude Dialogist* frameth this Argument following:

"That which comes in place of the Old Sab-
"bath, is commanded in the fourth Com-
"mandement.

"But the Lord's-Day is come in place of the
"Old Sabbath.

"Therefore the Lord's-Day is commanded in
"the fourth Commandement.

When the *Bishop* read this Argument, propounded with no little pride and ostentation by the *Dialogue broacher*, he admired *the ignorance and stupidity*

pidity of the Man. *For* the major Proposition, is so notoriously false and absurd, and refuted by so many instances, that hee is τυφλότερος λεβηρίδος [a], *as blinde as a Calves Kell*, who cannot discerne the rudity and falsity of it. *As for example:* The *Sacrament of Baptisme* succeeded, and came in place of Circumcision: *The Holy Eucharist* in place of the Legall Passeover: *Evangelicall Sacrifices* in place of Legall and Leviticall: *The Evangelicall Law*, in place of *Moses* Law.

If now one shall argue, *Ergo*, the Sacrament of Baptisme, is commanded by the Old Law of Circumcision: *and* the Sacrament of the Lord's Supper, by the Old Law of the Legall Passeover, &c. *shall* he not declare himselfe to be voyde of common understanding?

Although therefore the Lord's-Day came in place of the Old Sabbath day of the fourth Commandement; *Yet* it was not commanded or observed in the Christian Church, by authority of that Law: *any* more than Baptisme is command by the Law of Circumcision.

But now the contrary to that, which the Objector imagineth, *may* be concluded by this argument, namely:

That day, which comes in place of the Old Sabbath Day, is not commanded by the Old Law, but by some other new Law: *For these two dayes, differ in kinde, the one being Legall, and the other Evangelicall*; *now* even as that which is meerely Legall, is not commanded by the Law of the Gospell, but by the Old Law: *even* so that which is meerely Evangelicall, is not commanded

[a] τυφλότερος λεβηρίδος. Aiunt liberidem proprie significare membranam extremam, qua fœtus vaccarum obtegitur: in qua & ipsa vestigia duntaxat oculorum apparent.

ded by a precept of the Old Law:

But the observation of the Lord's-Day, considered as a particular Holy day, grounded upon our Saviour's Resurrection, is meerely Evangelicall, according to *Brother B.* himselfe [a].

Therfore the Observation of the Lord's-Day, is not commanded by the Old Law of the fourth Commandement.

[a] *H. B. Law and Gospell reconcil. p. 61. That which gave it a stampe of divine institution, was the Lord's own act, in blessing and sanctifying this Lord's Day, with his blessed and glorious Resurrection.*

❖❖❖❖❖❖❖❖❖❖❖❖ ❖ ❖❖❖❖❖❖❖❖❖❖❖❖

A. I remember the Treatiser confesseth, that the Apostles themselves at sometimes observed this Day as *Acts* 20.7. 1 *Cor.* 16.2. *pag.* 211.

B. At sometimes only? What? no oftner than he findes expressely mentioned? *This* is like him in Oxford, who in his Sermon sayd that the Iewes kept the Sabbath, but once in 40. yeares, during their abode in the wildernesse. This he gathered, because he found it but once mentioned: but he might have found it twise, if hee had looked well. So as this is a most beggerly kinde of reasoning.

How injurious an imputation is it to the Apostles, to say that they kept the Lord's-Day sometimes, *when as they taught and commanded* [b] others to observe it weekly,

as

[b] *This bold compassion powreth out his own fancies, & takes that as granted which is imposed, and to be proved much deeper. Read 1 Cor. 16. Neither did the Apostles... ...*

as hath beene noted ; *Did* Christian People immediately after Christ's Ascension observe this weekely day, and did not the Apostles themselves ? This is too grossely repugnant to good reason, to our Homily, and to the witnesses produced.

Answ. 1. The *Bishop's* words *pag.* 211. are, *The Apostles themselves at sometimes observed this day*, &c.

Now the ingenuous Reader must consider the reason, why the *Bishop* spake thus reservedly, which was : *Theo. Brab.* had objected against the Lord's-Day, *that it could not be proved by Holy Scripture, that the Holy Apostles constantly observed the Lord's-Day, or that they commanded the observation thereof, two weekes, or one Moneth together in all Christian Churches.*

In answer to this Objection, the *Bishop* held it not sufficient to cry out, this is too grossely repugnant to good reason, and to the *Homily*, and to *Doctor Andrewes, and it is impudent :* but if hee would speake to purpose, hee must confirme his answer, by testimonies of Scripture.

Now when he had searched with much diligence, hee could finde none such : *Therefore* hee carryed himselfe like himselfe, in affirming no more than hee was, without quirkes and cavills, well able to prove. It's an easie matter, *like a Potgun, to* blurt out paper shot : *but* if one have to deale with an intelligent adversary, he shall be sure to come off with disgrace, if he make a noyse only, and prove nothing.

2 The Objector saith: that it is an injurious imputation to the Apostles, to say, that they kept the Lord's-Day sometimes, when as they had taught Christian people immediately after Christ's Ascension to observe it generally in all Churches.

Now in this assertion, there is:

1 *Petitio principii*: for this Dictator, neither already hath, nor at any time hereafter will be able to demonstrate out of Holy Scripture, *That* the *Apostles presently, and immediately* after Christ's Ascension, commanded all Christian Churches to observe the Lord's-Day. *For the Apostles* themselves, and namely Saint *Peter* were not resolved of the cessation of all *Legall Ceremonies* presently after Christ's Ascension, *Act.* 10. 14.

2 *Vntill the Conversion of the Gentiles, the Christian converts* among the Iewes observed *the Old Sabbath Day*, and the Apostles joyned with them in their Synagogues, preaching the Gospell to them upon that day, *Acts* 13. 14. *They came to Antioch, and went into the Synagogue on the Sabbath Day, and after the reading of the Law and the Prophets, the Rulers of the Synagogue said unto them, Yee men and brethren, if yee have any word of Exhortation for the People, say on,* Chap. 16. 13. and Chap. 17. 2. *And Paul, as his manner was, went in unto them, and three Sabbath Dayes reasoned with them out of the Scriptures.*

3 Saint *Paul* was not called to be an Apostle of the Gentiles, at the very instant of time of
Christ's

Christ's Ascension, *and* yet he was the first of all the Apostles, who in holy Scripture (above twenty yeares after Christ's Ascension) is reported to have preached the Gospell, and broken bread upon the Lord's Day, *Acts* 20. 7. &c.

A. These two witnesses (*Bishop Andrewes*, and M^r. *Hooker*) and these instances, I perceive, come full home to the Homily, and D^r. *Andrewes* calls the Lord's-Day our New Sabbath.

Answ. I doe earnestly intreate the impartiall Reader to consider, *that* this Dialogue-former hath not one sound, or probable argument, in his whole Treatise, either to prove his owne *Tenet*, or to confute his Adversary; *His* only colour is (and this may mis-leade a weake and improvident Reader) to wit, certaine passages in the Homily, and in some moderne Authors of our Nation, which according to outward sound of words may seeme to favour him;

Therefore it must be observed:

1 The *greatest Doctors* [a] at sometimes, and before Errors and Heresies are openly defended, are not, neither can they be so circumspect in their writing, as to avoyd all formes and expressions, all sentences and propositions, all and every Tenet, which in after times may yeeld advantage to the Adversaries of truth, *but in Homilies, and Sermons*

[a] Aug. *de præd. sanct.* c. 14 Quid opus est, ut eorum scrutemur opuscula, qui prius quam ista hæresis oriretur, non habuerunt necessitatem in hac difficili ad solvendum quæstione versari, quod procul dubio facerent si respondere quibus cogerentur?

mons especially, Divines use to speake more freely, and not to handle Questions Scholastically, or in a precise Doctrinall way.

Before the Pelagian Heresie did arise, *not only many Greeke and Latine Fathers, but even great S. Augustine* himselfe [b] maintained some passages which savoured of *Pelagianisme*: *S. Chrysostome* [c] in some of his Homilies is very broad, in advancing the naturall power of Free-will to performe good workes. But after that hereticall spirits had vented their heterodoxall opinions: *Then Divines became more circumspect, and wary; and they punctually, distinctly, and exactly propounded their Doctrine.*

[b] August. d. Præd. sanct. cap. 3. Neq; enim fidem putavi Dei gratia prævenri, ut per illam nobis daretur quod posceremus utiliter: nisi quia credere non possemus, si non præcederet prædicantium veritas: ut autem prædicato nobis Evangelio consentiremus nostrum esse proprium, & nobis ex nobis inesse arbitrabar: *quem meum errorem, nonnulla opuscula mea satis indicant.* c. Chrys. *in Iob Hom. 17.* Hinc admoneri possumus, Deum suis in nos beneficiis, nostras non prævenire voluntates, sed à nobis incipiendum esse. *Sed cum nos prompto, paratoq; animo, ad suscipiendam gratiam exhibemus, tunc multas nobis offert salutis occasiones.* Sixt. Senens *Bibl. lib. 5. Annot. 101.* Dic dum cum Aniano, Chrysostomum interdum naturæ nostræ vires plus æquo extulisse, ex contentione disputandi cum Manichæis & Gentilibus, qui hominem asserebant, vel natura malum, vel siti violentia ad peccatum compelli. Hieron. *c. Ruffin. l. 2.* Certe antequam in Alexandria, quasi dæmonium meridianum Arius nasceretur, innocenter quædam, & minus caute loquuti sunt (*Clemens Alexandrinus & alii.*)

I shall now crave leave to apply the former passage to the present occasion.

Before there arose Controversie in our Church concerning the Sabbath, *or* at leastwise before the Controversie grew to an height, Divines spake and writ more freely: and *they were not alwayes so cautelous and circumspect, as to foresee the evill construction which Adversaries of truth might make of their writing and speaking.* But now when *the Sabbatarian Heresie* [d] for the ne-

[d] Aug. *d. bon. persev. cap. 20* Didicimus singulas quasque Hæreses intulisse Ecclesiæ proprias quæstiones, contra quas diligentius defenderetur Scriptura Divina, quam si nulla talis necessitas cogeret.

cessary

cessary observation of *the old Sabbath*, and a fanaticall opinion of some others for the observation of the Lord's-day in a more precise forme than the very Iudaicall Law it selfe obliged the *Iewes* to keepe the old Sabbath: *when*, I say, these errours sprang up, and were defended with an high hand, and obtruded upon the Church, *A necessity* was cast upon us to examine all such Positions as were the grounds of such errours; and to examine all termes and formes of speaking, which were incident to the Question in hand.

Now if upon evidence of truth we shall in some passages dissent from some men of note, living in this Church before us, or use other termes in our writing or disputing: *Nay, if we shall in some things have altered our owne former opinion and formes of speaking* e, we trust that godly Christians will not impute this unto us as an offence, but in their charity will judge us (as the ancient Church did Saint *Augustine*, to wit) that what we doe in this kinde, proceedeth from the care we have, in faire and perspicuous manner to maintaine and defend Truth.

e Cyprian. *Ep. ad Quirin* Nec debere unumquemq; pro eo quod semel imbiberat, & fervebat, pertinaciter congredi : sed si quid melius & utilius extiterit, libenter amplecti.

Non enim vincimur quando offeruntur nobis meliora. Aug. c. Crescon. *l. 3 c. 3.* Sicut laudabile est, à vera sententia non amoveri, ita culpabile est in falsa persistere, quam nunquam tenere prima laus est, secunda mutare: ut aut ex initio vera permaneat, aut mutata falsa, vera succedat. Aug. *d. bon. persev. cap. 21.* Propterea nunc facio libros, in quibus opuscula mea retractanda suscepi, ut nec meipsum in omnibus me secutum fuisse demonstrem.

In the last place our Reader must observe, *That* the Objector himselfe regardeth not the expresse or literall sense of the Book of Homilies; neither receiveth the same as the Doctrine of the Church of *England*, but only according to his owne private interpretation; *for* in his *Flea to an Appeale*, traversed Dialogue-wise, betwixt *Asotus*, *Babylonius*, and *Orthodoxus, pag.* 14. he declareth himselfe in manner following:

The Appealer had affirmed, *That* if a person justified, and consequently in the state of Grace, should commit any foule and malicious crime, *to wit*, Adultery [a], &c. *and* should continue in that sin a Moneth, a Yeare, or for a longer time, acting the same againe and againe, or as often as opportunity served: *That* then such a person ceased to be justified, and in the state of Grace, untill he had forsaken his sin; *for* no person can be justified and consequently be in the state of grace, unlesse he have remission [b] of his sin from God, *Rom.* 4.7. But there can be no remission of sin from God, unlesse a sinner [c] repent him of his sin, *Acts* 3.19. *Luc.* 13.5. *&* 24.47. *and* in offences of such quality as adultery is, there can be no sufficient repentance, unlesse the offender forsake his sin [d], *Pro.* 28. 13. *Esay* 1.16,17. *&* 55.7. *An Adulterer therefore continuing in his sin*, & committing the same as oft as opportunity serveth, *is not justified before God:* For *God* who calleth it an abomination in us Men to justifie the wicked, *Prov.* 17.15. cannot himself justifie any sinner continuing in his wickednes; and therefore every such sinner ceaseth to be justified,

[a] Aug. *in Iob. tr.* 41. Crimen est peccatum grave, accusatione & damnatione dignū. Cyprian *d. Iudic.* Adulterium, fraus, homicidiū, mortale crimen est. Bernard *d. Præcept. & Disp. c.* 13. Adulterium quocunque loco quocunque tempore perpetres, immo, turpe flagitium est, & criminale peccatum.

[b] Chrys. *d. Pœn. Hom.* 5. Remissio peccatoru fons salutis & pœnitentiæ munus. Pœnitentia medicamentum est peccatum extinguens.

[c] Amb. *Ep.* 76. Debet pœnitentia præ damno peccati, ut gratia possit aboleri. Tertul. *d. Bapt. c.* 10. Pœnitentia antecedat, Remissio sequitur. [d] Aug. *lib.* 50 *hom.* 2. Si etiam totum dares, & peccatum non desereres, teipsum desereres. *Id. d. Ecclef. Dogm. c.* 54. Pœnitentia vera est pœnitenda non admittere. Idem *d. Temp. Ser.* 7. Ista est vera pœnitentia, quando sic convertitur quis, ut non revertatur; quando sic pœnitet, ut non repetat. *Idem. de Civ. Dei. lib.* 21. *cap.* 25. Non sunt membra Christi, qui se faciunt membra meretricis, nisi malum illud pœnitendo esse destiterint, & ad hoc bonum reconciliatione redierint. Hier. *Ep. ad Sabinian.* Si peccato mortui fuerint, tunc eis remittetur peccatum. Quod quamdiu in peccato vixerint, non dimittitur.

untill

untill hee have repented and forsaken his sinne.

The *Author of the Appeale* (at this present *a learned and Reverend Bishop*) maintained the former Doctrine by the words of the Homily, *affirming that the Doctrine* delivered *in the Homily* was the Doctrine of the Church of *England, pag. li. 32.*

In answer to the former, *Brother B.* sets his glosse upon the Homily, saying ª, that *we are to measure the Doctrines of the Church of* England *by the line and rule of holy Scripture: and that we must not take the words of the Homily at the first rebound, according to our owne fancy, but so far as the same is consonant to the word of God,* pag. 14.

But if this Rule which the Dialogue Dauber hath approved, is authenticall; *then* we can see no reason, *wherefore* it may not be lawfull for us, as well as for him, to expound the words of *the Homily* in point of the *Sabbath*, according to the sense of holy Scripture. *And* if we may do this, *then* it is undoubtedly true, that it was not the intent of the *Homily* to make the 4ᵗʰ Commandement a Precept of the Law of Nature; or a morall Precept purely, intirely, and properly such.

Our request likewise is, that *Br. B.* would make a review of a confident Argument propounded by him against the Appealer in his Plea, *pag* 17. the scope whereof is: *That a Person once justified, and in the state of Grace, if afterwards he become an* Adulterer, *or wilfully commit any other the like crime or sin, and continueth therein, yet he still remaineth in the state of Grace, without any diminution of his faith, no not in the degrees.*

His Argument is as followeth; *A mortall Father*

ª *Plea to the Appeale.* Ib. *As neither the Church of England her self avoucheth, or concludeth any thing for Doctrine & matters of faith, but so far as is consonant to the word of God: so neither are we to measure her doctrines, but by the only line and rule of the Scriptures.* Ib. *For the Articles and Homilies of the Church of England, wee subscribed unto the indeed: but not to the private sense, which every particular man may put upon them.* Idem. Christ. Conf. & Compl. pag 82.

ther begets a mortall Son: So the immortall God can beget no Son, but he is immortall.

Now it is impossible for the immortall God to dye, no not for a moment.

Of this nature also is the Borne of God [a], he cannot fall away totally, that is, dye in his spirituall life, no not for a moment.

But upon the foresaid ground, Br. B. may proceed further, and conclude, that no person once regenerate, can possibly sin at any time, in thought, word, or deed, neither can hee die a temporall death. For if God Almighty, being a Father of the regenerate, hath begotten all his sonnes, in nature like himselfe, and it is impossible for God Himselfe, either to dye, or to sinne: Then it will likewise be impossible, for any Regenerate Persons to sinne, in thought, word, or deed, they cannot at any time covet or lye, or transgresse any Divine Law, neither can they dye a temporall Death.

The learned Author of the Appeale, beleeveth that Br. B. was pleased to act *Asotus* his part (although hee stiled himselfe *Orthodoxus*) when hee propounded the former Argument.

For although it is true, that an immortall father, begetting a son of the same nature and substance with himselfe, every such naturall sonne, must be immortall, like unto his naturall father (as appeareth in *the second person of the Trinity, according to his Deity* [b]) yet it is extreme false, and most absurd to affirme, that all such Persons as are the Sonnes of God, meerely by his Voluntary Election, free gift, or by Creation, or Adoption, and
so

---

[a] H. B. Plea to the Apeal. Now this being so cleare a proofe, if any places of Scripture seeme to be opposit, they are so onely in sound, not in sence.

[b] Aug. c. Faust. Manich. li. 3. ca. 3. Unicum filium habet Deus, quem genuit de substantia sua, de quo dicitur, cum in forma Dei esset, non rapinam arbitratus est, se æqualem esse Deo. Nos autem non de substantia sui genuit, sed fecit.

(95)

so farre as they imitate and obey him *, *Matth.*5. 45. doe partake the essentiall, and naturall proprieties and Attributes of God himselfe their heavenly Father. For *Adam* was the sonne of God by Creation, *Luk.* 3. 38. And *Infants baptized are regenerate with the Holy Spirit, and made the Children of God by Adoption*: and yet notwithstanding *Adam* by disobedience fell from grace, and beeame mortall: and all *Infants regenerate in Baptisme* are mortall, and many of these comming to yeares of discretion, by sinne and Infidelity fall away from the state of Grace, and Adoption a, received in their Baptisme.

Prosper *Aquitanicus* b, S. *Augustine's* Disciple and interpreter, saith as followeth: *Ex regeneratis in Christo Iesu, quosdam relicta fide & piis moribus apostatare à Deo, & impiam Vitam in sua aversione finire, multis (quod dolendum est) probatur exemplis.* Among those which are regenerate in Christ Iesus, that some persons by forsaking faith and good manners fall away from God, and end their wicked life in Apostasie, is proved, (the more is the pitty) by many examples.

* Id. *Serm. Dom in Mont. c* 45. Vnus naturaliter filius est qui nescit omnino peccare. Nos autem, potestate accepta, efficimur filii, in quantum ea quæ ab illo præcipiuntur implemus. *Id. in Psal.* 44. Ille creando pater: sed nos illum imitando filii.

a August. *Ep.* 59. Quod dicturus est de Infantulis parvulis, qui plerique accepto in illa ætate gratiæ Sacramento, qui sine dubio pertinerent ad vitam æternam, regnumque cælorum, si continuo ex hac vita emigrarent, simul ut crescere, & nonnulli etiam Apostatæ sunt.

b Prosp. ad artic. fals. impos. *cap* 7. Cyprian. *Ep.* 76. Nonnulli de illis, qui sant baptizantur, si postmodum peccare cœperint, Spiritu immundo redeunte quatiuntur: ut manifestum sit diabolum Baptismo fide credentis excludi, si fides postmodum defecerit, regredi.

A Sir you have abundantly satisfied me in this point, and, I suppose, every Rationall man, and true bred sonne of the Church of *England*: *and* surely I wonder so learned a man should commit so foule

an

an error, as not to search better into the Doctrine of our Church, so clearely expressed in the Homily.

Answ. In *the Bishop's Epistle* prefixed to this Treatise, and in the precedent examination of the Objections out of the booke of *Homilies*, the judicious Reader will observe this former babble of *Br. Asotus*, fully confuted, both by the expresse words of our Statute Law, and also by many other weighty arguments and authorities.

B. You need not wonder at it, wee have all known him to do as great a matter as that: for was not his hand to the approbation of a Booke in printe, (though afterwards called in by Sovereigne authority) which containes, and maintaines many, sundry Tenets both *Pelagian* and *Popish*, flat against the cleare Doctrines of our Church: and whereby he hath as yet made no publike recantation, to remove the scandall from the Church of *England*, and to satisfie so high an offence given.

Answ. One *H. B.* some few yeares past, vented an envious and illiterate Pamphlet, against the
Author

Author of the Appeale, and against *his Approver*, accusing them, that *they avow, approve, and stiffely maintaine grosse and grievous heresies, devised by the Devill*:

The principal, and most notorious of al the rest, he makes the Appealer's Tenet concerning *the losse of faith and justification: which one heresie* (saith he) *overthroweth the whole tenure & truth of the Gospel: it turneth upside down the very foundation of our salvation, it reviveth directly in part, & by consequence altogether, that wicked Heresie of the Pelagians*.

The *Appealer* in the Treatise, (which H. B. entertaineth with such foule *language*) affirmeth, that it seemed to him; *A justified person, by committing foule and wilfull sinne, might really fall away from grace, and cease to be justified*.

The 16. Article of our Churches Doctrine, and the words of our Homilies ᵃ seemed to him, to maintaine this position: and Saint *Augustine*, and his followers were of this judgement.

H. B. after much *prating and ignorant disputing*, comming at length to Saint *Augustine*, saith as followeth : *Saint Augustine is so copious in this point of perseverance* (to wit, that justified persons cannot fall away from grace, either totally or finally) *that I marvell that any man, who hath read St. Aug. of these points, would ever meddle with him in this matter, to wrest one mangled testimony, against so many pregnant proofes of truth*.

Now Br. B. was forced to this desperate assertion, because otherwise he must have beene proclaimed a *malicious Calumniator*, in accusing the Appealer of *Pelagianisme*, and *devilish Heresie*.

H. B. *Plea to an Appeale. Pref. to the Reader.*

ᵃ *The first and second part of the Sermon of falling from God, pag. 54. and pag. 57.*

For

(98)

For Saint *Augustine* was a professed Adversary to the *Pelagians*, and to all their devillish Heresies, and therefore if this most learned, and godly Father in his disputations against *Pelagians*, and their Adheres, expressely and constantly maintained, that some regenerate and justified Persons might *really fall away* from saving and justifying grace; then it is certaine that the said Tenet is not *Pelagian.*

Saint *Augustine's* Positions concerning the former question.

First, this *Holy Father* distinguished justified Persons, into two kinds or sorts, to wit:

1 Some of them are God's Children according to his secret and eternall *Predestination* [a].

2 Some justified persons are his Children, *propter susceptam temporaliter gratiam*, because for a time only, (namely during their perseverance,) they [b] are partakers of divine grace.

The first of these are God's sons, because according to his *eternall purpose* they are *predestinate* to the finall receiving the inheritance prepared for his Children.

The *Temporary* are not his Children according to his eternall *prescience* [c], and because hee foreseeth they shall not finally persevere, and obtaine the Crowne of everlasting glory.

Secondly, St. *Aug.* affirmeth of both these sons, the *Temporary*, as well as the *Perseverant* [d], that

---

[a] Aug. de Corrept. & grat. ca. 9 In iis praedestinatione futuri eorum, nondum sunt filii ejus.

[b] Ib. c. 8. Mirando ... modo, & quod sunt filii Dei qui... eos quos regeneravit in Christo, quibus fidem, spem dilectionem dedit, non ... perseverantiam.

Ib. ca 9. Filius suus non praedestinatus, Deus perseverantiam non dedit

[c] Aug. Ib. Non dixisset filios praescientia Dei Prosp. ad artic. fals. imposs... 7.

[d] Aug. de Bon. persev... Utrique vocati fuerunt, & vocationem sequuti: ut... ex impiis justificati, & per lavachrum regenerationis utrique renovati... Id. de Cor. & grat. ca. 6. Si aute... jam regeneratus & justificatus, in mala... sua voluntate relabitur, certe ille non potest dicere, non acceperam accepta gratia Dei, suo... Libero ... arbi... ... ...

that they were *called of* GOD, *and they followed or obeyed his calling*; *Vtrique ex impiis justificati*, both of them being naturally impious, were justified, and regenerate or renewed by the *laver of Regeneration*.

Thirdly, he teacheth, that *the temporary*, during the time of their perseverance, were *endued with faith working by Charity* [a]: *Acceperunt fidem quæ per dilectionem operatur*: They had received faith working by Charity: *They lived justly, and faithfully for a time* [b], They lived *piously with hope of immortality, not foiling their Conscience with foule crimes* [c]: *They heard the voyce of Christ, and obeyed it* [d]: Lastly, during the time of their perseverance, *Non simulaverunt justitiam*, They played not the Hypocrites, neither was their righteousnesse fained [e].

Fourthly, St. *Augustine* his Tenet was, that justified and regenerate persons of both kindes *have fallen away*, and *possibly they may fall away* from justificant grace. The *Predestinate* may fall away for a time, but so, as they shall undoubtedly by Repentance, and forsaking their sin, recover [f].

The *non predestinate* do fall away in such manner, as that they either perish in the act of their sin, or if they live, they fall into hardnesse of heart, and are never renewed by repentance.

Fifthly his Doctrine is, that if the *Temporary* and *non perseverant* had beene taken out of this

a Aug. de cor. & gr. ca 6. fide quæ per dilectione operatur. Ib. c. 8. cum qua Christi ad viverent dilectionem dedit. Ib c 13. In fide quæ per dilectionem operatur incipere vivere.
b Ca. 8 cu fideliter & pie viverent cum coluerit bona fide.
c Id. de Civ. Dei li. 11. c. 12. Quos videmus juste & pie vivere cu spe futuræ immortalitatis, sine crimine vastate conscientiam.
d Id. in Ioh. tr. 45. quandiu recte sapiunt, audiunt vocem Christi.
e Id. d. cor. & gra. c. 9. Deum coluerunt bona fide c. 8.
f Aug. de civ. Dei. li. 17. c. 8 c. Fausti Munich. li 3 & 88. d. Doctr. Christ. li 3. ca 21. in Psa. 126. In Iohan. tr. 66. et tr. 103. d. Bapt. c. Do. li 1. c. 11. d. cor. & gr. c. 6. & 7 & 8 & 13. Ad art salv. impos art 13. Hypognost. li 6 ca 7. Novimus aliquos etiam perfectos ex libore multorum annorum probos…

life by temporall death, before their *Apoſtaſie*, they muſt undoubtedly have beene ſaved.

But God Almighty, foreſeeing their voluntary *Apoſtaſie*, permitted them to prolong their dayes in this preſent evill world, untill they fell into damnable crimes, and continued in the ſame without returning into the ſtate of juſtifying grace [d].

[margin: d *Aug. d. corrept. & gra. cap. 8.* Reſpondent, li poſſunt, cur illos Deus, cum ſciret et pie vixerint, non tum de hujus vitæ]

periculis rapiat, ne malitia mutaret intellectum eorum. *Idem. d. Bon. perſev. cap* 9 & 10, & 13. *d. pec. mer. & remiſſ. lib.* 1. *cap* 21. *Id. ad Vital. Epiſt.* 107. Cur quidam non permanſerint in fide & ſanctitate Chriſtiana, tamen acceperint ad tempus hanc gratiam, & dimittantur hic vivere donec cadant, cum poſſint rapi de hac vita, ne malitia mutaret intellectum eorum, quod de ſancto infante utrum æt ue defuncto ſcriptum eſt in libro Sapientiæ, quæ ratio quiſq́ſ ut potuerit. *Idem d. Prædeſt. ſanct. cap.* 14. Quis audeat negare Chriſtianum juſtum, ſi morte præoccupatus fuerit, in refrigerio futurum? Item ſi dixerit juſtum, ſi a ſua juſtitia receſſerit in qua diu vixit, & in ea impietate fuerit defunctus, in qua non diu, immo unum annum, ſed unum diem duxerit, in pœnis iniquis debitas hinc iturum, huic perſpicuæ veritati quis fidelium contradicit? Porro ſi quæratur à nobis, utrum ſi tunc eſſet mortuus quando erat juſtus, pœnas inventurus eſſet an requiem, nunquid requiem reſpondere dubitabimus? Hæc eſt tota cauſa cur dictum eſt, raptus eſt ne malitia mutaret intellectum ejus. *Ibid.* Quare aliis concedatur ut ex hujus vitæ periculis dum juſti ſunt auferantur, alii vero juſti donec à juſtitia cadant, in eiſdem periculis vitæ productiore teneantur, quis cognovit ſenſum Domini? *Ib.* Cur autem hic tenuerit calutum juſtum, quem priuſquam caderet poſſet auferre, juſtiſſima omnino, ſed inſcrutabilia ſunt judicia ejus. *Idem ad Paulin. Ep.* 59. Non ſunt in iſta vocatione, qui in fide quæ per dilectionem operatur, etiamſi aliquantulum ambulant, non perſeveraunt uſq́ſ in finem: & ut pie potuerunt rapi, ne malitia mutaret intellectum eorum.

Sixthly, this *Orthodoxall Father* (according to the Tenure of holy Scripture) conſtantly taught, that *Light and Darkneſſe, Chriſt and Belial, Righteouſneſſe and Vnrighteouſneſſe, cannot cohabit at one time in one and the ſame ſubject*: and conſequently, that foule and wilfull ſins are not *compatible* with ſaving and juſtifying grace.

If any Chriſtian (ſaith he) *ſhall love an Harlot, and*

and adhere unto her, and be made one flesh with her, jam in fundamento non habet Christum, *He retaineth not Christ in the foundation* [a].

They are not lively members of Christ, who make themselves members of an Harlot, untill by repentance they forsake that sinne, and by returning unto good, reconcile themselves unto God.

He who lives in hatred or malice only with one Man, loseth God, and the benefit of his former good [b].

Covetousnesse is the root of all evill, and Charity is the root of all good, and these twaine simul esse non possunt, *cannot be together* [c].

Lastly, upon the former ground, hee deterreth faithfull Christians from denying the Faith in time of persecution, and from killing themselves in any case whatsoever, affirming that the same is Scelus inexpiabile, *an impardonable crime in all persons whatsoever:* & auferendo sibi presentem vitam, abnegant & futuram, *by destroying their present life, they deprive themselves of the future blessed life* [d].

But now quite contrary to this Doctrine of S. *Augustine* (according to H. B) a person once justified, and in the state of grace, although he *couple with an Harlot*, or live in envie or malice with his Neighbour; or be a Schismatick in the Church, and a Rebell in the Common wealth; or if he deny the Faith in time of Persecution; or to prevent worldly misery he shall *murder himselfe:* he neither falleth totally nor finally from grace; he sinneth not unto death [e], his faith remaines intire without diminution: *it faileth not, no, not in the degrees:* and if any places of Scripture

a Aug. d Civ. Dei. li. 2. cap. 25 & cap. 20.

b Id. d. spir. & anima. c. 58.

c Id. lib. Quinquag. Hom. Hom. 8

d Id. d. emendat. ad Consent. c. 6. & d. Civ. Dei. li. 1. c. 17. & c. 26. Enchirid. ad Laurent. ca. 70. & d. patient. c. 13. ad Gaudent. c. 18. & c. 19. Ep. 50 & 52. & 61.

e H. B. Plea to an Appeale pag. 16. & 17. & 25. & 55.

seeme to be opposite, they are so onely *in sound, and not in sense.*

Seventhly, S. *Augustine's* Tenet was: That because of the frailty and mutability of man's will, and by reason of perill of man's falling into sinne, (he being overcome by temptation:) no person ordinarily, or *without speciall revelation*, during his mortall life, which is a warfare on earth, can be infallibly certaine of his own finall perseverance: and God Almighty, to humble Man, and to move him to watch and pray, lest he fall into temptation; and to stir him up to worke out his salvation with feare and trembling, hath reserved the knowledge hereof in his owne secret Counsell [a].

[a] Aug. d. C. Dei. li. 11. ca. 12. Quilicet de suæ perseverantiæ præmio certi sunt, de ipsa tamen perseverantia reperiuntur incerti. *Quis* enim se in actione profectuq; justitiæ perseveraturum usq; in finem sciret, nisi aliqua *revelatione* fiat certus. Id. d. Bon. persev. cap. 1. Asserimus donum Dei esse perseverantiam, qua usq; in finem perseveratur in Christo. Finem autem dico in qua vita ista finitur, in qua tantummodo periculum est ne cadatur. Itaq; utrum quisque hoc munus acceperit quamdiu hanc vitam ducit, incertum est. Id. cap. 13. & cap. 22. De vita æterna quam filiis promissionis promisit non mendax Deus ante tempora æterna, nemo potest esse securus, nisi cum consummata fuerit hæc vita, quæ tentatio est super terram. Id. d. Cor. & gra. cap. 13. Quis ex multitudine fidelium, quamdiu in hac mortalitate vivitur, in numero prædestinatorum se esse præsumat, quia id occultari opus est in hoc loco, ubi sic cavenda est elatio, ut etiam per Sathanæ angelum, ne extolleretur tantus colaphizaretur Apostolus. Id. in Psal 41. Novi quia justitia Dei manet, utrum autem mea maneat, nescio. Terret enim me Apostolus dicens: qui putat se stare, videat ne cadat. Prosper d. voc. Gent. lib. 2 cap. 37. De nullo, ante ipsius finem, pronunciari potest, quod electorum gloria sit futurus, ut perseverantem humilitatem utilis metus servet, & qui stat, videat ne cadat.

Conclus. It is evident by the former Positions of S. *Augustine,* that his constant and expresse Tenet in his Confutation of the *Pelagians,* was: That some persons *really justified,* might afterwards bee overcome by temptations, and fall

fall away from saving and justificant grace.

And therefore *H. B.* is *mendacious* in accusing the *Appealer* of *Popery, and Pelagian Heresie*: for we trust, he will not honour *the Papals* so much, as to make S. *Augustine* one of theirs. And that cannot in any charitable construction be a *Pelagian Heresie*, which S. *Augustine*, the grand Adversary of those *Hereticks*, in his Answers and Confutations constantly maintained against them.

B. Yea, instead of recantation, I my self have heard him in open Court speake against both justification; that a Man might be justified to day, and damned to morrow; and against election of some to eternall life; and against the sanctification of the Sabbath; saying, I say there is no sanctification of the Sabbath, but Rest, Rest only. And therefore cease to wonder that this man should be so fearelesse, either privily to undermine, or apertly to oppugne the expresse Doctrines of our Church.

Answ. 1. It was the Tenet of S. *Augustine* a, and of the faithfull in his dayes, that *if a just person forsake his righteousnes, in qua diu vixit, wherin hee hath lived long, and shall depart this life in wickednesse, in qua non unum annum, sed unum diem duxerit*

a *Aug. d. Præd. Sanct cap.* 14.

duxerit, wherin hee continued not one yeare, but one day, *in pœnas iniquis debitas hinc iturum*, hee shall passe from hence into eternall punishment due to the wicked. *Huic perspicuæ veritati* (saith Saint *Augustine*) *quis fidelium contradicit?* what faithfull Christian contradicts this evident or perspicuous verity?

Now if the former doctrine was maintained for Catholike and Orthodoxall, in Saint *Augustine's* daies, then he, who saith, a man may be justified to day, and be in perill of damnation the next day [b], hath delivered nothing savoring of Pelagianisme, or repugnant to sound Doctrine, in the Article of Iustification.

2 *Br. B.* is false in saying, he hath heard his Adversary in open Court speake against *God's Election*; for the *Bishop* firmely believeth; That *God hath freely (without any merit of their owne) in his meere bounty and love, for the merit of Christ, elected all those to eternall life, which shall be glorified in the world to come.*

3 The *Bishop* truly affirmed, *pag.* 143. That the fourth Commandement of the Decalogue, according to the literall sence thereof; enjoyned not such spirituall, and Evangelicall duties, as *Theop. Br.* mentioned in his Objection; to wit, preaching of Christ crucified, and rayted from the dead: *Prayer to God the Father in the name of Christ: receiving Baptisme, and the Holy Eucharist:* But he maintaineth that the equity of the fourth Commandement, together with the Evangelicall Law, requireth not only rest from secular labour and negotiation, but also the performance of

spirituall

---

[b] *D. Overall, Confer. Hampt. Court. p.* 41. *Whosoever (though before justified) did commit any grievous sinne, as Adultery, Murder, Treason, and the like, did become ipso facto, subject to God's wrath, & guilty of damnation or were in state of damnation quo ad præsentem justitiam, untill they did repent.* Against which doctrine (he said) some had opposed, teaching: That all such persons as were once truely justified, although after, they fell into never so grievous sinnes, yet remained still just, or in the state of justification, before they actually repented of those sinnes: Yea, and although they never repented of them, through forgetfulnesse, or otherwise, yet they died saved without repentance.

spirituall and evangelicall duties, upon the Lord's-Day, and upon other Holy dayes and times, devoted by the Church to the service of Christ, *pag.* 143.

A. The Adversary in his Booke doth much except against, and cannot endure, that the Lord s-Day should be called the Sabbath Day. *And* I remember one passage in it, wherein he bequarrelleth. *H. B.* for saying, *that* the ancient Fathers did *ever* and *usually* call it the Sabbath Day.

B. Concerning that I have spoken with *H. B.* and hee saith he will answer and make good, what he hath said against his Adversary. *And* howsoever those words indeed, *ever* and *usually*, might give Advantage to the Adversary to carpe, *yet* being rightly understood, they may passe currant enough; *for* by *ever, usually,* hee meant that all the ancient Fathers, although they distinguish betweene the Lord's-Day, and the Iewes Sabbath Day, *yet* they ever took and observed the Lord's-Day instead of the Old Sabbath, and ever used it for the Rest day or Sabbath of Christians.

P *Answ.*

Answ. 1. The *Bishop's* words, *pag.* 201. are: *I have diligently searched into Antiquity, and observed in the Fathers, their formes of speech, when they treate of the Lord's-Day. And I finde it farre differing from the usuall language of the Fathers, to stile the Lord's-Day the Sabbath Day; And they by the name Sabbath either understand the Old Legall Sabbath taken away by Christ, Or the mysticall and spirituall Sabbath, which was tiped and represented by the Sabbath of the fourth Commandement.*

2 In the former passage the *Bishop* speaketh not of moderne writers, neither hath he denied, that any of these, (especially here in *England*,) have stiled the Lord's-Day, by the name of Sabbath, or Christian Sabbath: for his assertion, was onely concerning the Ancient Fathers *: *And therefore Br. B. fighteth with his owne shadow,* when he produceth moderne authorities, to confirme that, which concerneth not the point in question.

3 The *Bishop*, pag 205. makes cleare ostension, that *H. B. had falsified three places of* Saint *Augustine: And* (to prove himselfe an impudent Prevaricator) he had foisted in these words, *Hoc est Dominicum,* into Saint *Augustine's* very text. *Contra Adimant. Manich. Cap.* 15.

4 This *Br. B.* for his last refuge, propoundeth a miserable and ridiculous argument: to wit, *The Fathers observed the Lord s-Day in stead of the Old Sabbath:* Ergo, they ever, and usually, called the same, the Sabbath Day.

This argument may be paralleld with one like unto it: *The ancient Fathers observed the Sacrament*

ment of Baptisme instead of Circumcision: *Ergo*, the Ancient Fathers did ever usually stile the Sacrament of Baptisme, by the name of Circumcision.

✦✦✦✦✦✦✦✦✦✦✦✦✦✦✦✦ ✦✦✦✦✦✦✦✦✦✦✦✦✦✦

B. Saint *Augustine de temp.* Ser. 251. affirmeth: That the Holy Doctors of the Church have decreed to transferre all the glory of the Iudaicall Sabbath, or Sabbatisme unto the Lord's-Day, &c. We must observe the same from evening to evening, &c. that being sequestred from Rurall workes, and from all businesse, we may be vacant only for the worship of God: Thus we duly sanctifie the Sabbath of the Lord, &c. You see hee speaketh this not as his owne particular opinion, but as it was the Tenet of the whole Catholike Church, so as the whole ancient Catholike Church did not only observe, but call the *Lord's Day the Sabbath*, &c.

Answ. 1 This Sermon seemeth to be none of Saint *Augustine's*, as appeareth by the stile: *Nolite in Ecclesia verbosari, In Ecclesia garriunt & verbosantur. Cogant Presbyterum ut abbreviat Missam.*
2 The Author of this Sermon, requireth the

same

(108)

same Vacancie and sanctity, upon the *Birth dayes of Saints as he doth upon the Lord's-Day* [b].

3 He affirmeth that the Holy Doctors of the Church translated the glory of the Iudaicall Sabbath, upon the Lord's-Day [c]: *And* therefore he could not, without contradiction, ground the Observation of the Lord's-Day, upon the letter or expresse words of the fourth Commandement.

4 He makes the Sabbath of the fourth Commandement and the Lord's-Day, two distinct, and diverse dayes of the week; and when he saith, *sic quoq; rite sanctificamus Sabbatum Domini*, &c. He useth the word *Sabbath* in a mysticall and analogicall sence, and not in a Legall, or literall signification.

5 It is an untruth, that Saint *Augustine* [d] makes it the common stile of the Catholike Church, *to call the Lord's-Day the Sabbath*: for he was so far, either himselfe from stiling the Lord's-Day the Sabbath, in a proper or ordinary course of speaking, or from approving this forme of speech in others, that hee holdeth it *inept and insolent* to give Iudaicall names and Appellations, to Persons or things, which are Christian or Evangelicall: and hee gives a reason hereof, because by such ambiguous formes of speaking, a Christian might seeme to professe that which is repugnant to true Christianity.

[b] *Idcirco, fratres mei, non fervorus modestum, in Dominicis diebus, & in natalitiis Sanctorum, divino studere cultui.*

[c] *Ideo Sancti Doctores Ecclesiæ, decreverunt omnem gloriã Iudaici Sabbatismi in illum transferre, &c.*

[d] *Aug. ad Asellic. Epist. 200. Cum quisq; isto modo fuerit verus germanusq; Christianus, utrum etiam Iudæus aut Israelita dicendus sit merito quæritur? Quod quidem si non in carne, sed spiritu hoc esse intelligitur, non debet ipsum nomen sibi imponere, sed spiritualiter ejus retinere, ne propter ambiguitatem vocabuli, quum non diceret quotidiana locutio, illud profiteri videatur, quod est inimicum nomini Christiano. Non debemus consuetudinem sermonis humani inepta loquacitate confundere, & inepta insolentia, & si dici potest, imperita scientia.*

B.

(109)

B. Hilary. *Prolog. in Pſal.* Though in the ſeventh day of the week both the name and obſervance of the Sabbath be eſtabliſhed : *yet* we on the eighth day, which alſo is the firſt, doe enioy the feſtivitie of the perfect Sabbath.

Anſw. The Queſtion is not; Whether the Ancient Fathers have at any time ſtiled the Lord's-day, a Sabbath, *in a myſt.call and ſpirituall ſenſe,* that is, a day wherein Chriſtian people ought to abſtaine from ſin. For in this ſenſe they have ſtiled *every day of the Weeke* b, wherein Chriſtians reſt from ſin, a Sabbath, *pag.* 203, 204.

But whether the Fathers did ever and uſually name the Lord's-day *the Sabbath of the fourth Commandement* in a proper and literall ſenſe; *The* Biſhop hath proved the Negative, with ſo many pregnant teſtimonies of the Fathers, *pag.* 202. *that* no reaſonable perſon can take any juſt exception.

b Clem. Alex ſtrom.l.5.c 6. Qui perfectus eſt ratione, operibus, cogitationibus, perpetuo hærens verbo Deo, naturali noſtro Domino, ſemper agit dies Domini, & nunquam non habet Dominici. Tert. c. Iud. c 4. Vnde intelligimus magis Sabbatizare nos ab omni opere ſervili ſemper debere, & non tantu ſeptimo quoque die, ſed per omne tempus Chriſt in Mat. ho. 40. Quid Sabbato opus eſt illi, qui per totã vitam agit ſolennitatem? qui præceptorum minutias, virtutes obſervat, & colit?

A. Dr. Wh. denies that Chriſt upon the day of his Reſurrection reſted from the work of Redemption.

P 3   *B.* I

B. I conferred with *H. B.* about this, because it much concernes him to quit this Question; *seeing* on Christ's resting on that day, he grounds the Sabbatisme of it, as agreeable to the fourth Commandement: *And* in my judgement, if he can evince and cleare it, *it* will prove unanswerable.

And he tels me, that he hath in two severall *Treatises in Latine* [a] against *Theophilus Brab.* fully cleared it, *and* removed all Objections and Cavillations, that either *Theophilus Brabourne,* or *Francis White,* have or can bring to the contrary; *and he purposeth to do the like to D. Wh.*

And he made it very cleare to me, that Christ's rest from the worke of Redemption from sinne on the Crosse, and from death in the Grave (which was a branch of that worke) began not till his Resurrection; as for his Ascension, that was into the place of rest, but his Resurrection was into the state of rest.

As for *D. Wh.* his Objection with *Theophilus Brabourne,* That Christ laboured on that day, *H. B.* shewes it to be absurd and ridiculous, seeing Christ arose with a body glorified,

---

Marginal notes:

Maintaining your own principles, that the fourth Comandement is purely & simply morall, and of the Law of Nature, it will be impossible for you, either in English or in Latine, to solve Theoph. Brab. his objections.

In Brabin's words [it] could was no action on that day: but the word labour, is of Br. B. his owne coining.

glorified, and impassible: So *as* his actions that day could not bee called a labour, that thereby the new Sabbath should bee broken.

Answ. 1. Our Saviour began his Rest from those workes of Redemption, by which he made paiment of a price by his bloud for our sins [c], upon the latter part of *Goodfriday*, immediately upon his saying *Consummatum est, and giving up the ghost*, *Iohn* 19.30. *Heb.* 10.14. *Then* he continued in his Grave and Bed of rest the *Sabbath-day following*: *upon* the *Sunday* he began his operations of *Application* of the fruit and benefit of his Passion: *and* he did no more rest or cease from those actions upon *Sunday*, than he did forty dayes after.

2 Christ rested as fully upon the Munday, Tuesday, and upon every day following the day of his Resurrection, from all his *afflictive* and *satisfactory Passions*, as he did upon the *Sunday*. If therefore it were granted that Christ began his Rest upon Sunday, *it* must be confessed, that he continued his Rest and Cessation from *Redemptive actions* every day after: *and* so the *Sunday* was not the only day or time of his Rest.

And if it shall be further objected, *that even as notwithstanding the Lord God ceased, and rested from the worke of prime Creation, on every day of the weeke following, as much as he did on the first Sabbath; yet the seventh day was made the Sabbath, because the Lord on that day began his Rest: Therefore*

[c] *Liturg. didst give thine only Son IESUS CHRIST to suffer death upon the Crosse for our redemption, who made there by his owne oblation of himselfe once offered, a full, perfect, and sufficient Sacrifice, oblation & satisfaction for the sinnes of the whole world, &c.* Ordering of Priests: *after hee had made perfect our redemption by his death, &c.*

fore because Christ began his rest upon Sunday, the same must bee the Christian Sabbath of the fourth Commandement.

Our answer is, that God's resting or ceasing from the worke of Creation, did not ordaine the *Seventh day* of the Week to be the *Sabbath day* [a]: for it was God's expresse Commandement and Law which did this, and his Rest was onely a *Motive* (and that meerely in his owne good pleasure) of sanctifying that particular Day.

But now concerning the Lord's-day, we finde no such expresse and particular divine Law or Commandement *in holy Scripture*; and therefore Christ's resting from all his Penall sufferings, upon the day of his Resurrection, cannot make that day of the weeke a particular *Sabbath-day* of divine institution, unlesse some such expresse divine Law as the *Iewes* received for their *Sabbath*, can be produced.

But if the Objector will obstinately contend, that *the Resurrection of Christ* in it selfe containeth a *Mandatory Law* to observe the *Lord's-day*, let him first deliver a true definition of a Law, *and then prove that the said definition belongs to the Resurrection of Christ.*

A Law (say the Iurists) *is a Precept of a Superiour being in authority, containing a Rule or Measure of things to be done, or not to be done.*

But neither this, nor any other true definition of a Law [b], or of a Commandement, agrees to the Resurrection of Christ.

Therefore the Resurrection of Christ may be a *motive or cause impulsive*, inducing the Church to make a Law, but it is not of it selfe any formall Law.

And if our Saviour's Resurrection hath the force of a Law to ordaine the day on which hee rose, to be the Sabbath of the fourth Commandement. *We can observe no reason, why the day of his Ascension*[b] *on which he entred into his eternall Rest, should not likewise have the force of a Law, to ordaine Thursday to be a Christian Sabbath: because* if our Saviour's beginning to rest shall make *a Sabbath: certainly* the perfecting of his Rest should much more do the like.

[b] Walæus d. Sab. p. 158. Quod si serium Christum eo die refurrexisse, ac proinde eundem ad cultum suum, Resurrectione sua sacrasse, necessarium argumentum non habet. Quia Christus diem Jovis suo in cælos ascensu consecrarit, nec propterea tamen sequitur, cum singulis septimanis, in memoriam rei tus ejus esse observandum: *Nam* licet hæc Christi resurrectio argumentum præbuerit Ecclesiæ Apostolicæ, ut hunc diem cæteris ad habendos conventus præferret. Non tamen sequitur Christum hoc suo facto eundem diem in eum finem instituisse.

3 This Objector *falsifieth the Bishop's words foisting in the word Labour,* instead of the word *Action*, and then he brayes in his rude tone, *absurd and ridiculous*.

But every reasonable Creature knowes there may be *action without labour*, as appeareth in the actions of *God Almighty*[c]; and in the actions of the *blessed Angels*, and of the *glorified Saints* in Heaven. And therefore bold B. is a *false brother*, in corrupting and perverting the *Bishop's* forme of words; *and* the *Bishop's* assertion is most true, That our Saviour having finished all sorrow and labour upon his *Passion-day: He* was in action upon his *Resurrection-day:* and he was in *Action* likewise forty dayes after.

[c] Aug. d. Gen. lib. 1. cap. . Non itaq; in ejus cessatione cogitetur ignavia, desidia, inertia, sicut nec in ejus opere, labor, conatus, industria. Novit quiescens agere, & agens quiescere.

Q B. Lest

B. Leſt neither the Church of *England* in her publike Doctrine, nor the pious workes of her grave and learned Sons may perhaps ſatisfie the Adverſarie's importunity; *yet* I hope the writings of his more pious, and no leſſe learned Brother, *D. Iohn White* (and thoſe alſo both republiſhed and vindicated by *Fran. White* from the Ieſuites Calumnies, *White dyed black, &c.*) will a little qualifie him.

How *D. Iohn White* doth not only call the Lord's-day the Sabbath-day, as once, *Sect.* 38.1. and twice, *Sect.* 43. *digreſſ.* 46.6. But he alſo condemnes all profane ſports and recreations on that day, and among the reſt Dancing for one. *And* for this he alleageth the example of the Papiſts, as the moſt notorious Sabbath-breakers in this kinde.

A. Doth he ſo Sir? This ſeemes ſtrange to me, that ſo great a Clerk as *Fran. White* ſhould ſo far forget himſelfe, as not to remember what his Brother hath writ; *Surely* if it be ſo, it will be a cooling-Card, and
no

no small disgrace to his *Lp.* when so worthy and reverend a Brother shal be brought as a witnesse against him. But I pray you, for my better satisfaction, relate to me the very passages and words of *D. Iohn White.*

B. I will, *in digress.* 46. the Title whereof is, Naming certain points of the Popish religion, which directly tend to the maintenance of open sinne, and liberty of life: now among many foule and profane practises (as he cals them) this he notes for one, namely, the profanation of the Sabbath, in these words: *That* they hold it lawfull on the Sabbath-day to follow Suits, Travell, Hunt, Dance, keep Faires, and such like. This is that hath made Papists the most notorious Sabbath-breakers that live.

And *Sect.* 38. *n.* 1. He saith: Let it be observed if all disorders bee not most in those parts among Vs, where the people is most Pope-holy, &c. And for mine own part, having spent much of my time among them, this I have found, that in all excesse of sinne, Papists have beene the Ring-leaders in riotous Companies, in drunken meetings,

meetings, in seditious assemblies and practises, in prophaning the Sabbath, in quarrels and brawles, in Stage-Playes, Greenes. Ales, and al Heathenish customes, &c. Thus this reverend Divine *Candore notabilis ipso*, whom all the Iesuiticall smoak out of the bottomlesse pit cannot besmeare or besmudge, or dye blacke with all their black mouth'd obloquies.

A. Surely these are very pregnant passages. *And it makes me tremble to* thinke, and amazeth me, *How one White* is so contrary to another: *As* also how the Libertinisme dispensed with now a dayes on the Sabbath, tendeth to bring Vs Protestants to be like to the Papists, in their prophane times, in taking up their Heathenish, savage, and barbarous manners and customes.

Answ. This *rude Dialogist hath a Palsie in his braine*; which causeth him to tremble: *For* the matter it selfe affoordeth no occasion of any such passion.

For there is not any contradiction, between the two brethren in their Doctrine: *For the one brother called the* Lord's-Day, the Sabbath in a mysticall sence: *And the other brother* saith, *it is not the Sabbath of the fourth Commandement,* in a literall and proper sence. *One brother* condemneth

Papist.

Papists for using prophane, ungodly, savage, and heathenish pastimes upon the Lord's-Day: *The other Brother* maintaineth that some kinde of pastime and recreation, namely *such as is not Vicious, either in forme, or quality, or in Circumstance,* may be lawfully used, upon the Lords-Day.

But the Objector (as his manner is) wasteth many words, but avoydeth, and declineth the true state of the question.

✦✦✦✦✦✦✦✦✦✦✦✦✦✦✦ ✦ ✦✦✦✦✦✦✦✦✦✦✦✦✦

B. Me thinkes the very reading of the fourth Commandement every Lord's-Day might stop his mouth : *saving* that he hath found out many inventions to elude the nature and property of this Commandement, as *pag.* 158. 159. &c. which I hope *H. B.* will meete withall.

Answ. It was one of *Theoph. Brabourn's* arguments *ad hominem*, to prove, that we are to observe the literall Sabbath of the fourth Commandement, because this Commandement is read in the Church every holy day, and after the reading thereof, *we beseech God to incline our hearts to keepe that Law.* For that Commandement enjoyned the observation, of the *seventh day Sabbath,* to wit the same Sabbath, which the Old Testamen established, and the Iewes observed.

Now this argument being popular, and plausible. *The Bishop* is perswaded, he did good service

vice, in solving the same upon true grounds. *And because this Objector is not able (holding his own Principles) to give any solution, or satisfactory answere to it:* He should not *like the Dogge in the manger,* have barked against others, and done nothing himselfe.

B. The twentieth Injunction of *Queene Elizabeth,* He also perverteth, *whiles* he confoundeth the Lord's-Day with other Holy dayes, which the Injunction doth clearly distinguish: for that liberty, which it dispenseth with, touching worke in Harvest time, *is* not spoken of the Lord's-Day, or Holy day, as is there called and set alone by it selfe: *but* of Holy and festivall dayes only of humane institution.

A. I thanke you for this observation.

Answ. In which words doth *the Injunction* clearely distinguish *the Sunday* from the other Holy dayes, in respect of *labour in Harvest?* bold *Br. B.* cease to prate and out-face, and prove what you say: otherwise none will credit you, but *Goslings* of your owne brooding.

1 The *Queenes Injunction* speaketh in generall, of all holy dayes in the yeare, and it setteth down no difference betweene *Sunday,* and the other Holy dayes, concerning *working in Harvest.*

2 Queene

2 Queene *Elizabeths Injunction*, was taken Verbatim out of an *Injunction* of the same quality of *King Edward the sixth*, which was grounded upon the Statute, *Quinto & Sexto*, of *Edward the sixth*.

Now in this Statute,

1 The Sunday is made one of the ordinary Holy dayes of the yeare. *All the dayes hereafter mentioned, shall bee kept, and commanded to bee kept Holy dayes, and none other: that is to say, all Sundayes in the yeare, the dayes of the feast of Circumcision, Epiphany,* &c.

2 In this Statute, no special priviledge (for abstinence from necessary labour) is given it more than the rest. *Statute* Edward sixt, *provided alwayes, and it is enacted by the authority aforesaid, it shall be lawfull to every husbandman, labourer, fisherman,* &c. *upon the Holy dayes aforesaid in harvest, or at any other time of the yeare, when necessity shall require, to labour, ride, fish, or worke any kinde of worke, at their free wills and pleasure, any thing in this act to the contrary in any wise notwithstanding.*

3 In our present Liturgie, the *Sunday* is ranked among the other Holy dayes, in these words: *These to bee observed for Holy dayes, and none other: That is to say all Sundayes* in the yeare: *the dayes of the feast of the Circumcision of our Lord Iesus Christ: of the Epiphanie: of the Purification of the blessed Virgin,* &c.

4 The Homily formerly cited by the Objector, granteth liberty to people to exercise some labour on the *Sunday* in time of great necessity: and *Queene Elizabeth's Injunction* (agreeing with
ancient

ancient Imperiall Lawes ᵃ) specifieth one kinde of bodily labour, to wit, *working in harvest*. *Therefore* the Homily by labour understands not on'y bodily workes of *absolute necessity*, such as are mentioned by the Objector, to wit, about scare-fires, and invasion of enemies: but all labour in generall which is of urgent necessity, and which was not in those times prohibited by Civill or Ecclesiasticall Law.

A. I am occasioned to aske your judgement of those passages of his touching Recreations on that day, in which argument, he hath spent many leaves.

B. But without any good fruit. And as his discourses are hereupon large, so they require a large refutation, which I hope. *H. B.* will performe.

He distinguisheth Recreations into two sorts: 1. Honest and Lawfull; 2. Vicious and unlawfull, &c.

I note *his pitifull enterferings, by equivocations, contradictions* ᵇ, and the artifice of his purest naturall wit, in spinning a curious webbe of so fine a thred, as wherwith, though he may thinke to cover himselfe, yet it is pervious, and penetrable to every eye. *Answ.*

ᵃ Cod. Justinian. li. 3 Tit. 12 §. 3. Constant. ᵃ Epi. do. Omnes Judices, urbanæq; plebes, & cunctarum artium officia venerabili die solis quiescant. Rura tamen politè arata rura exhibeantur; quoniam frequenter evenit ut non aptius alio die frumenta sulcis, aut vineæ scrobibus mandentur, ne occasione momenti pereat commoditas cælesti provisione concessa.

ᵇ Let the *Judicious Reader* examine, by what *Arguments*, this *bladering beast* confirmes his rude accusation.

Answ. Whosoever shall reade the Treatise with impartiall judgement, will perceive that the *Bishop* in his Doctrine concerning Recreations, hath proceeded plainely, distinctly, and without equivocations or contradictions.

For. 1. He delivereth a definition of *Recreation* in generall, out of approved Authors, *pag.* 229.

2 He divideth *Recreations* into two kindes, to wit, into honest, and lawfull, and into such as are vicious, and unlawfull.

3 He defines these two species of *Recreations*, approoving the first kind, if they be used in due time, and with due circumstances: and condemning the latter upon all dayes and seasons.

But it seemes *this sonne of confusion is* offended, because the *Bishop's* Treatise concerning *Recreations* is so cleare, and exact, that he can finde no defective passage in it, on which he might fasten his *envious jawes*.

B. If I might bee *bold* ᵃ, I would aske him what he thinkes of promiscuous meetings of wanton youth in their May-games, setting up of May-poles, dancing about them, dancing the Morice, and leading the Ring-dance, and the like, unto which Dr. *Wh.* in the former passage, *pag.* 266. doth not obscurely point as it were with

You have superlative boldnesse but little truth and honesty.

R   the

the finger: *Are not these obscene or lascivious and voluptuous Pastimes?*

Answ. 1. This Momus deales like one *Vrbicus* in Saint *Augustine*: *Who* wanting Arguments to prove, *That* Christians were obliged to make the Sabbath of every weeke a fasting day, *fell* into a bitter invective against luxurious feasting, drunken binquetting, and lewde drinkings [a].

Brother B. is destitute of firme Arguments, to prove that all bodily exercise, and civill recreation is simply unlawfull, upon any part of the Sunday: *and* therefore he imitates that *Sectarian*, and declaimeth against lascivious and prophane sports and pastimes.

Now his Adversary *maintaineth no Recreation, which is prophane and lascivious, or which is vicious* in quality or circumstances, either upon Sunday [b], or upon any day of the Weeke, *Page* 229, &c.

2. Whereas the envious man demandeth, *what* wee thinke of *promiscuous meetings* of wanton youth, *setting up May-Poles*, &c.

Our answer is, *that* when' hee hath proved by sound arguments, such meetings and pastimes as the lawes of our kingdom, and the Canons of our Church, have permitted (after that the Religious offices of the day are performed) to be in quality or circumstance, dishonest or vicious, we must proclaime them to be unlawfull at all times, *but* especially upon the holy day [c].

B.

---

a Aug. *Ep.* 86. Cum cum argumenta deficiunt, quibus probet Sabbato jejunandum, in luxurias convivarum, & temulenta convivia, & nequissimas ebrietates invehitur, quasi non jejunare, hoc sit inebriari.

b Clem. *Apost. Const.* li. 5. ca. 9. Neq; in Dominicis diebus qui sunt dies lætitiarum, permittimus, vobis, quicquam inhonestum loqui, aut agere.

c B. Ely. Treat. p. 230. *If they bee used upõ the Lords Day, or on other festivall dayes, they are sacrilegious, because they rob God of his honour, to whose worship and service the Holy day is devoted: & they defile the soules of men, for the clensing and edifying whereof, the Holy Day is deputed.*

B. *I note how poorely he playes the Divine or Doctor*, by giving indulgence or more liberty to such as have quesie stomacks, and cannot digest those wholesome meats, which God's word, and all sound Divines and Doctors doe prescribe [a], &c.

Give Man a power thus to dispense with part of the Lord's-day, which is an incroachment upon the fourth Commandement, according to the Doctrine of our Church; *and* why may not Man assume unto himselfe a power (as the *Pope* doth) to dispense with Servants and Children, by allowing them some time, wherein they shall bee free from the Controle of their Masters and their Parents.

[a] *This Goose-quil antiquum obtinet: for he gaggles only, but produceth no sentence of Gods word truly applyed, nor one sound Divine or Doctor, who is adverse to the Bishop's Tenet.*

Answ. If there be no Divine Law prohibiting people to use honest and sober recreation upon some part of the Holy-day, then he is no *poore Divine or Doctor*, which yeeldeth such liberty to people, as God hath not denyed them.

But there is no Divine Law written or unwritten, prohibiting people to use honest and sober recreation upon some part of the Holy-day.

Therefore hee that yeeldeth such liberty to

R 2   people

people is no poore Divine or Doctor: But hee which upon false grounds denieth it them, is a *proud Pharisee*.

2 They which grant liberty to Children and Servants to disobey their Parents and Masters, take upon them power to dispense with a Divine Law, which is properly morall, and of the Law of Nature.

But they that grant licenseto Christian people, to use sober and honest recreation upon some part of the Holy-day, dispense with no Divine Law, either Morall, Naturall, or Positive.

Therefore the Objector's comparison is betweene things which are altogether unlike.

B. Our Treatiser doth miserably abuse the Scripture, and so turne the grace of God into wantonnesse: for he saith, *p.* 257. The Law of Christ is sweet and easie, *Mat.* 11. 30. *And* his Commandements are not grievous, 1 *Iohn* 5. 3.

Answ. He abuseth not the Scripture, who expoundeth and applyeth the same rightly.

But the Bishop hath expounded and applyed the two Texts of Scripture, *Matth.* 11. 30. and 1 *Iohn* 5. 3. truly and rightly:

Therefore the Objector is a false accuser, in saying the Treatiser hath abused the Scripture.

The

The Assumption is proved in manner following:

The Bishop delivered this Proposition: *All Divine Evangelicall Ordinances necessary to the salvation of every Christian, are possible with ordinary diligence, and likewise with comfort to be observed:* for the Law of Christ is sweet and easie, *Mat.* 11. 30. and his Commandements are not grievous, 1 *Iohn* 5. 3.

Now the foresaid Texts are truly expounded, and they do fully confirme the Bishop's Proposition.

Therefore the Dialogue-dauber is a *rude Blatterant* [a] in saying, the Treatiser hath miserably abused the Scripture.

[a] Hieron. ad *Ripar.* Quicquid amens loquitur, vociferatio & clamor est appellandus.

✦✦✦✦✦✦✦✦✦✦✦✦✦✦✦✦ ✦✦✦✦✦✦✦✦✦✦✦✦✦✦✦

B. And what then? is Christ's Law so sweet and easie, as that it gives indulgence to profane libertinisme? *This* is to make the Gospell a sweet Fable, as that Atheisticall Pontifician said.

Answ. 1. Christ's Law is so sweet and easie, as that it commandeth no externall service, or duty necessary, *Necessitate medii* to be performed by all Christians, which they may not by the assistance of Divine Grace be able to performe with ordinary diligence and comfort [b]. *This* Position is confirmed by the Bishop, *pag.* 257. both by sentences of holy Scripture, and by testimonies of ancient Fathers.

[b] Araus. *Concil. ca.* 25. Hoc etiam secundû fidem catholicã credimus, quod accepta gratia per baptismum omnes baptizati Christo auxiliante & cooperante quæ ad salutem pertinent, possint ac debeant (si fideliter laborare voluerint) adimplere.

And

And from hence it is consequent, that it is no sin, much lesse no mortall crime, equall to Murder, Adultery, and Theft (as the Novell Sabbatizers preach, *pag.* 235.) for Christian people to use some intermission from religious and spirituall actions, and likewise some recreation upon some part of the Lord's-day: *and* they are not obliged during the whole day (which according *to the Sabbatarian Tenet containeth 24. houres*) to forbeare to speake any words, or think any thoughts, or to performe any workes or actions, which concerne either pleasure or profit, (read *pag.* 249.) because it is morally impossible for them with comfort and ordinary diligence to continue 24. houres together, in spirituall and religious exercises and meditations.

2 The Law of Christ condemneth all *profane libertinisme*: but why doth Br. *Asotus* stile such re-creations as neither is vicious in forme, quality or circumstance, by the name of profane liberty? And other recreation than this the Bishop maintaineth not, either upon Sunday, or upon any other day, *pag.* 219.

3 The Bishop intreateth *Br. B.* to resolve him, whether it is not a Doctrine of *Libertinisme* to animate Christian people in disobedience of *lawfull Authority*; to teach them it is a branch of their Christian liberty, to be their owne guides in point of Religion; to deprave, or to neglect the Common Service, and other Duties, enjoyned by the precepts of the true Church, whereof they are members, to maligne *Ecclesiasticall Governours*, and to proclaime them *Veines of the*
Pope

Pope: and to be of a *Papall Spirit*, if they presume to instruct the inferiour Clergie in point of Religion: To be quarrell godly and learned persons, who comply not with the new Sect, in their fanaticall asseverations: and to censure, and controle all things, which are not sutable to their owne groundlesse and senselesse traditions.

Now in good earnest you *Br. B.* many judicious men are of minde, that the fomenting of these humours in Christian people by Doctrine or example, is a more proper act of profane libertinisme, than such bodily exercise and recreation, as the Lawes of our Kingdome and State have permitted.

※※※※※※※※※※※※※※※

B. I observe a very improper, and so an untrue speech, where hee saith: *if they should (upon Puritan Principles) restraine them wholly from all repast.* Who (I pray you) doth restraine the people, from all repast on the Lord's-Day? Or is prophane sport a repast, to feede the rude Vulgar? it seemeth so: and liberty to youth is as their meate and drinke.

Answ. It appeareth by the Law of the Sabbath, *Exod.* 23. 12. That one end and use thereof was; the refreshing of the people upon the seventh day, after six dayes toile and labour: And
the

the old Sabbath, and other Festivals, were *Dies Latitiæ*, dayes of mirth and rejoycing: and sober and honest recreation, upon some part of the old Sabbath, was prohibited by no Divine Law, *pag. 237.*

Now if in the time of the Gospell, Christian people upon Principles borrowed out of the *Talmud*, and the Rule of *Pharisaicall Tradition*, should be surcharged with such rigid Ordinances, as are imposed by *Novell Sabbatarians, pag. 235, 236. 249, 250.* and be wholly restrained from all recreation, upon any part of the Holy-day, *One end of the Holy-day, should be destroyed*: and Christian people must be deprived of that liberty which God and nature have granted: and from hence it will be consequent, that the Holy-day, instead of a day of *Refreshing*, shall become a day of *Oppressing* people with an heavier burden, than in right ought to be laid upon them: and this would make the Holy day more unwelcome than the plough-day: and besides, it might engender in peoples mindes, a distast of their present Religion, and manner of serving of God, *pag. 266.*

This passage highly displeaseth *the Dialogue-broacher*; but instead of solid answer and confutation: First, he carpeth at the forme of speech, affirming that it is *improper*, but wherein he declareth not; then he saith it is *untrue*, this likewise is easily said, but impossible to be proved. After this he equivocates, saying; *Who (I pray you) do restraine the people from all repast on the Lord's-day*, that is, who restraineth people from eating and drinking on the Lord's-day? And lastly, he declineth

clineth the true state of the Question; for whereas his owne Tenet is *Vniverfall*, to wit, that all civill recreation is unlawfull upon the Sunday: in his difputation hee oppofeth fome kindes of bodily exercifes and recreations, which feeme to him to be lafcivious, profane, and really vicious in their proper forme and quality.

✤✤✤✤✤✤✤✤✤✤✤✤✤✤✤✤✤✤✤✤

B. Pag. 266. He faith, fome Recreations (not prohibited by our Lawes) our religious Governours allow upon Holy-dayes. And *Pag.* 232. Civill recreation not prohibited in termes, neither yet by any neceffary confequence from the Law, cannot bee fimply unlawfull. And *pag.* 231. No juft Law, Divine, Ecclefiafticall, or Civill, doth totally prohibit the fame.

To this I reply, that thofe fports fore-fpecified, are prohibited, by Law both Divine, Ecclefiafticall, and Civill. 1. By Divine Law, as *Rom.* 13.13. *Gal.* 5.21. 1 *Pet.* 4.3. &c. 2. By Ecclefiafticall Lawes and Councels, &c. 3. By juft Civill Lawes, &c.

Anfw. 1 It is an infallible verity, and confeffed by the *Dialogue-forger* himfelfe, that nothing can bee vicious or finfull, unleffe it bee prohibited

S   expresly

expressely or virtually, by some just Law ^c, Divine or Humane.

But sober and honest repast, recreation, or pastime, upon some part of the Holy-day, is prohibited by no Divine Law, nor by any Ecclesiasticall or Civill Law of our State and Church.

Therefore sober and honest recreation, &c. upon some part of our Holydayes, is not vicious, sinfull, or unlawfull.

Now the Objector in his reply declineth (as his manner is) the true state of the Question, and inveigheth against certaine *particular Exercises and Recreations*, excepted against by some learned Divines, and which have beene prohibited by publike authority in foraigne Nations.

"But the Bishop in his Treatise proceeded no
"further concerning recreations, than is before
"expressed: to wit, that *such as are neither vici-*
"*ous in forme, quality, or circumstance, may lawful-*
"*ly be used upon some part of the Holy day, if they*
"*shall be permitted by lawfull authority.*

"And the maine reason of his forbearance
"was, because in the first part of his Treatise, he
"undertooke to deliver no other Doctrine con-
"cerning the old Sabbath & the Lord's-day, but
"such only as seemed to him, both to be *Ortho-*
"*doxall, and also Catholike:* and therefore he de-
"clined the Question concerning Pastimes and
"recreations *in their particular,* (leaving the same
"to a publike determination of the Church and
"State) by reason there now is, and in former
"times hath beene diversity of opinion, among
"godly men, concerning the quality of such par-
"ticulars.   "And

c *Aug. d. pec. mer. & remiss. l. 2. c. 12. Neq; peccatum erit, si non divinitus jubeatur ut non sit. Br. B Dialog. p 12. A sin it cannot bee, but as a breach of one of God's holy Commandements; for where there is no Law, there is no transgression.*

"And if *Br. B.* esteemeth those bodily exerci-
"ses and recreations, to be profane and vicious,
"which his *gracious Majestie in a royall Edict*, per-
"mitteth his Subjects, with *sundry cautions, limi-*
"*tations, and provisoes* [a]: let him in his Disputa-
"tion and Objections proceed humbly and mo-
"destly (as becommeth a loyall Subject, addres-
"sing himselfe to his Soveraigne) and propound
"weighty arguments, sufficient to convince those
"who are of contrary judgment: but in the mean
"time let him abstaine from scandalous & abu-
"sive passages against his Majesty; and likewise
"against other persons, who being Subjects, are
"perswaded that it is their duty to be obedient
"to Royall Authority, *unlesse such things be com-*
"*manded as are, Aperte contra Deum*, that is, *in ve-*
"*ry deed*, and not in some mens opinion only, re-
"pugnant to the Law of Christ [b].

[a] 1. *None to bee permitted, which were prohibited by any former Lawes, or by any Canons of the Church.*
2. *None to be used but after the end of all Divine Service and afternoone Sermon.*
3. *The said recreations are prohibited to all persons, both Recusants and Conforme in Religion, who are not present in the Church at the Service of God.*
4. *Every person must resort to his own parish Church, and be there present at Divine Service.*
5. *Each Parish by it selfe, to use the said recreations after Divine Service: and no Meetings, Assemblies, or concourse of people out of their own Parish, on the Lord's-day.*

[b] *Promptuar. Iuris tr. 9. cap. 5. n. 68.* In dubio semper præsumitur pro justitia legis, donec non expresse appareat pro contrario: & sic in dubio tenentur subditi obedire. *Bernard. d. præcept. & dispens. cap. 12.* Quicquid vice Dei præcipit homo, quod non sit tamen *certum* displicere Deo, haud secus omnino accipiendum est quam si præcipit Deus. *Ib.* Ipsum quem pro Deo habemus, tanquam Deum, in his quæ *aperte* non sunt contra Deum audire debemus.

S 2   *B.* Edition

B. Edition second of his *Dialog. pag.* 28. *Enough* to settle me, and every good subject of his Majesty in this beliefe, that the *Declaration* for sports, and the urging of it, to be none of his Majesties act : *but* a meere plot of some Popish Priests, and Prelates, to eate out, and tread downe Religion, and to Usher in Popery, Atheisme, and prophanenesse into the Church.

Answ. If *Lucifer* himselfe should preach or write, that wicked and lying fiend could hardly utter any thing more false, seditious or scandalous, than is contained in the former passage.

1 His sacred Majesty now is, and hath ever been so gracious and Religious, as that his princely care and desire is, to have his Subjects under him, to leade a quiet and peaceable life, in all godlinesse and honesty : and therefore it is farre from him, to be guided, or over-ruled by Popish Priests and Prelates in any matters of Religion.

2 If his Majesties declaration shall be duely examined, it tendeth to the repressing of Popery : for no subjects are thereby permitted to use any sports or pastimes upon the Holy day, but such onely, as shall duely frequent the Church, and bee present both at Divine service, and at the Sermon.

3 The

3 The Royall edict granteth no liberty to any subjects, though conforme in Religion, to use any sports or pastimes upon the Sunday, formerly prohibited by the Lawes of the kingdome: nor yet untill all the Religious offices of the day shall be finished, and duely performed: and therfore it can be no meanes to usher in Atheisme and profanenesse into the Church.

4 Such manner of Preaching and Writing, as this venomous Dogmatist useth in his fiery Sermons, and in this and in some other of his unlicensed Pamphlets, are very apt and ready meanes to impoison his Auditors and factious Disciples, with disloiall thoughts against his Majesties government, and with desperate intentions against his subordinate Ministers, and consequently to usher in rebellion and sedition, into the Church and State.

✦✦✦✦✦✦✦✦✦✦✦✦✦✦✦✦ ✦✦✦✦✦✦✦✦✦✦✦✦✦✦✦✦

A. I remember the *Bishop* of *Elye's* maine argument (as I understand, and apprehend) to prove his recreations to be lawfull on the Lord's-Day, is: because honest and necessary labour is lawfull on that day.

Answ. The *Bishop's* maine argument, to prove some pastime and recreation upon the *Lord's-day*, to wit, such as is not vicious in quality or circumstance to be lawfull, and which is used after such time as the *religious offices* of the day are performed, is: because such recreation is not prohibited by any Divine Law, naturall or positive, nor by any necessary inference from the same.

B. But, as I conceive, the Parallell doth no way hold, as will appeare clearely by these particulars.

1 Honest labour is necessary on that day in respect of necessity only, it being unlawfull, if not necessary, and may bee deferred: but there is no necessity of sports and pastimes, unlesse in some instant dangerous infirmity of the body, and some moderate recreation be prescribed by the Physitian.

2 Honest necessary labour is lawfull in the foresaid sense, on any part of the Lord's-Day, even in time of Divine Service and Sermons: But so are not sports and pastimes by the *Bishop's* owne confession.

3 Labours absolutely honest and necessary, as to quench fires, to make up Sea breaches, to defend the assaults of enemies,

attending

attending persons dangerously sicke, are lawfull all the day long, and for many successive Lord's-Dayes together: but sports and recreations may not bee used all the Lord's-Day long, nor on every part of the day, nor many dayes together.

Answ. 1. It is false, that no labour may bee used upon the Lord's-Day, but such only as is of *absolute necessity.* For then it must have beene unlawfull for the *sicke of the Palsie,* and the *lame man at the poole of Bethesda,* after they were healed, to have carryed their beds upon the Sabbath day, *Mark.* 2. 11. *Ioh.* 5. 9, 10. for this was not a worke of absolute necessity, but such as might have been deferred untill the evening of the Sabbath, or untill the next morning.

2. The Netherland Divines handling this question, speak as followeth: *Non audemus improbare, quod post Arelatense Concilium Constantinus in suis constitutionibus tempore pluvio, aut alio necessitatis casu, permittit, ut messes, & vindemia, etiam Die Dominico colligantur:* We dare not disallow that, which after the Councell of *Arles,* Constantine the great in his Imperiall constitutions permitted people in rainie weather, and in other cases of necessity, namely in the time of Harvest, and Vintage, to gather in their Corne, and Wine upon the Lord's-Day.

Answ.

B. But againe, admit that sports, and pastime and recreations are not expressely inhibited within the letter of the Law by these generall words, no manner of work, but only by consequence; yet it followeth not, that honest labour is more unlawfull than honest Recreations, as they are termed: For the *Bishop* and Fathers generally conclude, that rest from sinne is the chiefe thing commanded, and sinne it selfe the principall thing prohibited in the fourth Commandement, yet neither of them is commanded or prohibited within the words of this Precept. Therefore sports and pastimes by the same reason may bee more prohibited by it on the Sabbath, than labour, though not expressed. For *prophane Atheisme* is more unlawfull, at least more hainous, than the worshipping of false Gods; yet this last only is expressed in the very letter of the Law: So *Perjury* is more hainous than meere taking the Name of God in vaine, in ordinary discourse, and common swearing: *Sodomie, Incest,* and *Buggery*

gery, more odious sinnes than Adultery, or Fornication, though the other bee only within the intention of the Law, and by way of consequence prohibited by the 1. 3. and 7th. Commandements; the latter by the expresse letter and words thereof.

Answ. That which is directly, formally, expressely, literally, or by *a necessary, and immediate inference* prohibited by any Law, is ordinarily more unlawfull, than those things which by a remote & *probable inference* only are concluded to be repugnant to the Law.

The sins mentioned by the Objector, *Atheisme, Perjury, Buggery*, &c. are not only prohibited by necessary inference, and by the intention of the speciall precepts of the Decalogue, but also by the Law of nature, and by other expresse Negative Precepts, delivered in the Old and New Testament.

But whereas corporall labour was expressely, and in literall termes prohibited the Iewes, upon the Legal Sabbath-day: Honest and sober Recreation upon some part of the Lord's-Day, in such manner as the *Bishop* maintaineth the same, is prohibited neither by the expresse words of the 4th. Commandement, nor by any formall and necessary illation, from the words and sentences of that Commandement; nor yet by the Law of nature, nor by any negative precepts of the Old or New Testament.

T   Therefore

Therefore if bodily labour expressely and literally prohibited by the fourth Commandement, was, notwithstanding that prohibition, in many cases lawfull among the Iewes: Then honest and sober recreation, such as is neither vicious in quality nor in circumstances, being neither expressely, nor virtually prohibited or condemned by any Divine Law, naturall, positive, or Evangelicall, must be held to bee lawfull, untill the Opposers thereof shall bee able to make it evident by demonstrative reasons, that the same is repugnant to some divine Law, according to all, or some of those formes, which are before expressed.

❖❖❖❖❖❖❖❖❖❖❖❖❖❖❖ ❖ ❖❖❖❖❖❖❖❖❖❖❖❖❖❖

A. There remaineth yet one thing to be cleared, and that is about the judgement of the reformed Churches beyond the Seas, which the Opposite Author pleadeth to be all for him.

B. It's true, and I cannot *but smile*, when I thinke of it: That they which make no bones even in open Court to vilifie the prime pillars of those Churches, yea and to nullifie the Churches themselves, as if they were no true *Churches*, as having no lawful Ministers, because no Prelates to put them in orders; should notwithstanding daigne
to

to grace them so much, as to call them in, and to account them competent witnesses in the cause. *But a bad cause* [a] *is glad of any Patron, or Advocate to plead for it, though the Clyent have openly stigmatized him for a Rascall.* But what stead will the reformed Divines stand him in ? *Certainly in the point of sports and Recreations, they will utterly faile him, yea and disclaime him too. In the point of the Institution of the Lord's-Day, indeed, and the Obligation of it to Christians, a great part is for him, though the better part* [b] *is for Vs, this is confessed of Vs.*

[a] *How can that be esteemed a bad cause, which is confirmed by the common and consentient testimony of the most godly & learned Divines, both Ancient and moderne?*

[b] *Br. B. should have named some of those, which he accounteth the better part; for he is so precipitate and impudent in his affirmations, that judicious persons can give no credit to his own bare word.*

Answ. The *Bishop* in his Treatise hath made cleare ostension, that his Tenet concerning *the Sabbath and Lord's-Day*, is consonant, 1. To the Vnanimous sentence of Primitive Antiquity. 2. To the Doctrine of the Church of *England*, testified, and authorized by statute Law. 3. To the common Vote of the best learned Doctors of the reformed Churches [c] beyond the Seas.

The former Remonstrance hath produced two effects: 1. It hath given a mortall wound to *Br. B.* and to his Assistants, by declaring, that they are solitary, and singular in their Sabbatarian Tenet. 2. It hath yeelded full satisfaction to all judicious, honest, and godly Readers concerning this question.

[c] The *Augustane*, and *Helvetian* Confessions. *Melancthon: Calvin: Bucer: Bullinger: Peter Martyr: Musculus: Beza: Zanchius: Chemnitius: Visinus: Brentius: Hospinian: Hemmingius: Parcus: Herbrandus: Marbichius: Zepperi: Battus: Walaeus: Rivetus: Poliander: Gomarus: Thysius: Gualter: Piscator: Zegedinus: Steckelius, Heamanus, & alii.*

But the *Dialogue-Barker*, perceiving his cause to be desperate, in his obstinacy, neverthelesse, *spurneth against the prickes*, and proceedeth rudely and wildely in manner following:

1 He introduceth his interlocutory Assistant, one *Br. A.* who scratcheth his *fellow Mule*[a], and prateth in manner following: *You have so fully cleared this point about Recreation, from all the Subterfuges of him, that hath so moyled himselfe, to make something of nothing, &c.*

But wherein hath *Br. B.* cleared the point, *&c?* Hee hath alleadged some Decrees of Foraine States and Churches, which nothing concerne the *Bishop's*-Tenet: for they doe not so much as intimate, that all bodily exercise, and Recreation, and namely such as is neither vicious in quality, nor in circumstance, nor yet prohibited by the present state wherein people live, is simply unlawfull, or morally evill upon some part of the Holy day.

2 *Br. B.* Himselfe, to manifest his gravity, saith, *I cannot but smile*, &c. But besides his merriment, the *ridiculous man* uttereth no word, or sentence, savouring of truth, or sounding to reason: For,

1 Vpon the matter he confesseth, that the positions of the *Sunday Sabbatarians* here in *England*, are singular, and different from the common sentence of other Churches; for otherwise to what purpose serveth his speech, *pag. 6. The Church of England* (to wit *Br. B.* himselfe, and his owne Sabbatarian Allies) is *more cleare, and sound in the point of the Sabbath, than any Church in the world*;

for

[a] Mutuū muli scabunt: dictum, ubi improbi & illaudati se vicissim mirantur & prædicāt.

for it is as cleere as the Noone-day, that the Orthodoxall part of the Church of *England* accordeth with the Primitive Fathers, and with the Schoole Doctors, and with the best learned in the Reformed Churches; and renounceth the temerarious Doctrine of *H. B.* and of other Novell Teachers, concerning the Sabbath.

2 Whereas this Objector denies us the suffrage of Reformed Churches, pretending that some amongst us have vilified their prime Pillars, &c.

Our Answer is, *That this man doth not alwayes write or preach Gospell* a: for quite contrary to his report, we reverence and much respect, all learned and godly Divines, in what Church soever they live, or teach: yea, although in some Theologicall Questions wee take liberty (upon just reason) to dissent from them.

But admit the Doctors aforesaid were adverse to us, and we to them in many more Positions, than indeed we are; yet notwithstanding it might be lawfull for us to use their Testimony in all Questions, wherein they maintaine *Catholike and Orthodoxall Verity* b.

S. *Paul* used the Testimony of *Heathen Poets* in matter of truth, notwithstanding they were enemies to Christian piety c: and Christians likewise use the Testimony of *Iewes* and *Rabins*, concerning the number and integrity of the Bookes of Canonicall Scripture. S. *Augustine* used the Testimony of Saint *Cyprian* against *Donatists* and *Pelagians* d, who was adverse to him in the point of *Rebaptizing*. *Tertullian, Origen, Lactantius,* &c. had their errours: yet they that use their

a Hieron. *ad Iulian. Diacon.* Mendacia faciunt ut nec vera dicentibus credatur.

b Iren. *li.4 ca.14.* Vera & contradictioni minime obnoxia est probatio, quæ ex dictis adversariorum elicitur.

c Chrys. *in Gen. Hom.* 57. Infidelium & adversantiū religioni testimonia, majorem habent fidem. Et hoc est ex omnipotenti sapientia Dei, ut inimici veritatis fiant ipsi testes veritatis. August. *c. Petilian. Don. li.2.c1.* 30.

d Aug. *d. Bapt. c. Don. l.2.c.1.& l. 3.c.11.& l.4.c.1. & l 6.c 7. c Crescon. Gram. l.3.c 1. d. pradest. sanctor. c.14. d. pec. mer. & remiss. l.3 c.5.c Gaudent. l.3.c.1. Epist.*107.

T 3 testimony

testimony (when they speake divinely) were never as yet censured, by any sober or conscientious Writers, as maintainers of *a bad cause*, or bringers in *of Rascals to be their Advocates.*

✦✦✦✦✦✦✦✦✦✦✦✦✦✦✦✦✦✦✦✦✦✦✦✦✦✦

B. Certainly in the Point of Sports and Recreations, Reformed Churches will utterly faile him; yea, and disclaime him too, &c.

For the Ministers of the Seventeene Provinces reformed, and the neighbouring Churches in *Germany*, petitioned the States of the United Provinces, for the reformation of the manifold profanation of the Lord's-day.

Answ. The Bishop maintaineth not, but opposeth and condemneth all profanation of the Lord's-day. And as for honest and sober recreation, the best Divines of the United Provinces, approve the same upon some part of the Lord's-day.

The *Divines of Leidan, in Synopsi purioris Theologia, Disp.* 21. write as followeth: *Neq; tamen omnis recreatio hic prohibetur, ut quæ etiam inter fines Sabbati est: scilicet quæ divinum cultum non impedit, & sacris peractis, honeste, decenter, moderate, & sine scandalo & offensione fit. Nevertheless all bodily recreation (upon the Lord's-day) is not here*

here prohibited, because the same is one of the ends of the Sabbath: namely, such bodily exercise and recreation, as is no impediment to Divine worship, and which is used in honest, decent, and moderate fashion, without scandall or offence, after such time as the sacred and religious offices of the day are performed.

And in like manner *Walaeus* himselfe, (whom the Objector citeth) *de Sab. cap. 6. pag.* 131. *Vltimo quaeritur an recreationis, aut oblectationis opera fidelibus Sabbato sint concessa?* Recreationis *quaedam opera, hoc die esse concessa, non ausimus negare: quia Deus inter fines Sabbati hoc quoq; refert,* Exod. 23. 12. *Vt respiret,* (Iunius *vertit, ut recreetur) filius ancillae tuae. Et Christus ipse die Sabbati convivium adiit,* Luc. 14. *Et sane cum dies Sabbati fuerit festus, refert quoq; Laetitiam Caeli, hominis recreatio, atq; animae & corporis vires reficit, quemadmodum sapiens inquit,* Prov. 17. *Animus laetus medicinam facit, spiritus autem fractus exsiccat ossa. Atq; ideo etiam in Ecclesia Apostolica, Agapae erant institutae, translata (ut videtur) ex conviviis sacrificiorum Veteris Testamenti, ad* φιλαδελφίαν *mutuam testandam, & honestam recreationem usurpanda,* 1 Cor. 14. 20. Iude v. 12. *Imo & diebus Dominicis, ad gaudium propter memoriam resurrectionis testandam, jejunare in Ecclesia Primitiva, nefas fuit.* Aug. Epist. 86. ad Casulinum.

We dare not deny some kindes of recreation to bee lawfull upon the Lord's day: for God himselfe makes the refreshing of the sonne of the Handmaid, and of the Stranger, one of the ends why the Sabbath was ordained, *Exod.* 23. 12. And *Iunius* translates the word refreshed (וינפש) by recreated: Also *Christ* himselfe upon the Sab-

Sabbath-day went to a Feast, *Luke* 14. 1. And forasmuch as the Sabbath is a Festivall day, honest recreation upon that day, is a represent of heavenly joy: and according to the Wiseman's saying, *Prov.* 17.22. A merry heart doth good like a Medicine. Also in the Apostolicall Church, certaine Love-Feasts, called *Agapa* (being translated from Feasts used at Sacrifices in the old Law) were ordained to testifie brotherly love among Christians, and for the exercise of honest recreation: and upon the Lord's-day, to the end Christians might testifie their rejoycing for the memory of Christ's Resurrection, it was held a nefarious thing in the Primitive Church, to make that day a fasting day, as S. *Augustine* sheweth, 86. *Ep. ad Casulanum.*

Rivetus in Exod. 20. ^a *Honest recreations which refresh the spirits, and cherish mutuall society, ought not to be excluded from the solemnity of that day.*

^a Honestæ tamen recreationes quæ spiritus refocillent, & mutuum alant consortium, à solennitate illius diei non sunt excludendæ.

* * *

A. Sir, I heartily thanke you for your sweet conference, which I could be content might last yet a whole Summers-day: But the Day now bidding us farwell, leaves us to bid one another good night.

B. And so good night to you Brother.

A. And to you also good Brother.

Answ.

Answ. After a due and impartiall Examination of the former Dialogue, the Bishop protesteth once againe, that he hath observed no one passage in it, which meriteth any approbation: *And therefore Brother A. is fallen in love with his owne shadow*, when he stileth the same *a sweet conference* [a].

But let not *Brother Asotus* deceive himselfe: for his Dialogue is neither *sweet, nor savoury*, either in matter, or in forme; *but* very rude, wilde, malicious, and factious.

The maine Position of this Dialogue, to wit, *That the Bishop's Treatise of the Sabbath, overthroweth the Doctrine of the Church* of England, *&c.* is confuted in manner following:

1 The Doctrine of the Church of *England* concerning the Lord's-day, and all other Holy dayes, is the same at this present, it was in the raigne of *King Edward the* 6th, and in the raigne of King IAMES, *Anno primo.*

But the Bishop in his Treatise consenteth with the Doctrine, concerning the Lord's-day and other Holy dayes, maintained by Statute in the raigne of *King Edward the* 6th, and in the raigne of King IAMES, *Anno primo. Ergo,*

The Bishop in his Treatise, hath not overthrowne the Doctrine of the Church of *England*, concerning the Lord's-day and other Holy dayes.

2 The present Doctrine of the Church of *England*, concerning the old Sabbath, and the Lord's day, is the same which *the Fathers of the Primitive Church* received from the *holy Apostles*, and which *they taught Christian people in ancient time*, *pag.* 13.

[a] Ambros. Ep. 40. Vt filii etiam deformes delectent; sic etiam scriptorem indecores sermones sui palpant. *Lud. Vives.* Sicut pueri complectuntur & exosculantur specula in quibus imaginem sui aspiciunt, &c.

But

But the Bishop in his Treatise maintaineth the same Doctrine, which the *Primitive Fathers* received from the *Holy Apostles*, and which they taught Christian people in ancient time. *Ergo*,

The Bishop in his Treatise hath not overthrowne the Doctrine of the Church of *England*, concerning the old Sabbath, and the Lord's-day.

3 The present Doctrine of the Church of *England*, concerning the old Sabbath, and the Lord's-day, is the same which is commonly maintained by all *Reformed Churches* in Christendome.

But the Bishop in his Treatise, consenteth with all the Reformed Churches, in their common Doctrine of the old Sabbath, and of the Lord's-day, *pag.* 271. *Ergo*,

The Bishop in his Treatise hath not overthrowne the Doctrine of the Church of *England*, concerning the old Sabbath, and the Lord's-day.

4 That the *Homilies* appointed to be read in the Church of *England*, must not alwayes bee expounded according to the sound of words, but according to the Line and Rule of holy Scripture, is the Tenet of *H. B.* in his *Plea to an Appeale*, *pag.* 14.

The Bishop in his Treatise, hath expounded *the Homily*, of the Time and Place of prayer, appointed to be read in the Church of *England*, according to the Line and Rule of Holy Scripture; and according to this sense and exposition, nothing is delivered in the *Homily*, repugnant to the Bishop's doctrine, concerning the old Sabbath, and the Lord's-day. *Ergo*,

The

The Bishop in his Treatise hath now overthrowne the Doctrine of the Church of *England*, contained in the *Homily, of the time and place of prayer*.

Brother B. in his Dialogue hath these remarkable Passages following.

1 The Tenet of the Dialogist is, *That* the 4th Commandement of the Decalogue, delivered in this forme of words: *Remember that thou keepe holy the Sabbath-day, &c. The seventh day is the Sabbath of the Lord thy God, in it thou shalt doe no manner of worke, &c. The Lord rested the seventh day, &c.* commandeth in expresse termes, the religious observation of the Lord's-day: *and* the same is a commandement of the Law of Nature.

Now from hence it is consequent: 1. *That Saturday and Sunday*, being two distinct and severall dayes of the Weeke, if the Commandement be naturall and expresse for the one, it cannot be naturall and expresse for the other, unlesse the one day were named, expressed, or described in the same, as well as the other.

2 That the *Iewes* were obliged to the religious observation of the *Saturday* by the Law of the fourth Commandement, which was *Positive* in respect of that day: and Christians are bound to keepe holy the *Sunday*, by the very same Commandement, as by the Law of Nature.

V 2   Now

Now all judicious men confesse, that *the 4th. Commandement concerning keeping holy the saturday, was a Positive Law: Therefore* we desire Br. B. to cleare this contradiction: to wit, how it is possible that the Law of the fourth Commandement, concerning *Saturday*, being *Positive*, *The* same Law (according to his Tenet commanding *Sunday*) can be *Naturall*.

Againe, let this *bould Bayard* resolve Vs, how the observation of the Lord's-day, can be said to be expressely commanded in the fourth Precept of the Decalogue, when *Saturday* only, and no other day is expressed, either by the words of that Precept, or is concluded from the words or sentences thereof, by any formall or necessary illation.

Lastly, let him resolve Vs, how we may rightly conclude from the expresse words of the fourth Commandement, that *Sunday is* to be kept holy by that *Law: For* if this man will argue rightly, hee must proceed in this or the like manner. The fourth Commandement literally and expressely, enjoyneth the Observation of *Saturday* : and *the Precept concerning Saturday is Legally Positive*: Therefore Christians must observe *Sunday*, by vertue of such a Law as was *Legally Positive* for keeping of Saturday.

Gentle *Br. B. licke over your Calfe* once again, and please not your selfe, nor abuse your Reader with such absurd Bulls, and contradictions [a].

[a] Chrysost. in 1. Corinth. Ho. 38. Nihil est errore magis imbecillum, suis ipsis alis implicatur, nec oppugnatione aliunde opus habet, transfigit ipse se.

A second Passage of Brother B.

Vnlesse the keeping the first Day of the weeke for Sabbath bee commanded, the Divine Authority of it will not appeare (saith Br. B.) *for only God's Commandement bindeth the Conscience.*

> H. B. Dialog manuscript cited in the Bishop's Treatise of the Sabbath, pag. 89.

But no Divine Commandement is expressely delivered in the Old, or New Testament concerning the Religious Observation of the Lord's-Day.

Therefore if *Br. B.* his first proposition is true, and if hee bee not able to produce some Divine Commandement out of the Scripture, for the Religious Observation of the Lord's-Day: *he* must (if he adhere to his owne principles) be compelled to grant *Theoph. Brabourne*, that the observation of the Lord's-Day, is an act of superstition, and will-worship.

A third Passage of Brother. B.

There can be no Ceremony at all in the Law of the fourth Commandement, because Saint *Paul* reckoned the Sabbath Day, among the Ceremonies of the Old Law, *Colos.* 2. 16. And all the Primitive Fathers ranked the Sabbath and Circumcision in the number of Legall Ceremonies.

> H. B. Dialog. pag. 15.16. It were not wise to set a Ceremony, in the middest of morall precepts: It is a principle, in God there can be no ceremony, but all must bee eternall: and so in his Image, which is the Law of nature and so in the Decalogue.

A fourth Passage of Brother B.

The Primitive Fathers did *ever, and usually* stile the Lord's-day the Sabbath day of the 4th. Commandement, in a proper, and literall sence. *The* reason;because sometimes (but yet very seldome) They named it *Sabbatum,* in a *mysticall, and analogicall sence,* that is, an Holy day, on which Christian people must have a speciall care, to abstaine from sin.

A fift Passage of Brother B.

Because the Lord's-Day succeeded, and came in place of the Old Sabbath: Therefore the Observation thereof is commanded by the particular Law of the Old Sabbath: *As if* one should say, *Baptisme* succeeded and came in place of *Circumcision: Ergo* it is commanded Christians, by the Old Law of *Circumcision*.

A sixt Passage of Brother B.

The *Bishop's of England* may not use the Testimony of Divines of reformed Churches, because they dissent from them in some Theologicall questions; *As if* one should argue: *Protestants* may not use Saint *Augustine's* testimony against *Pontificians or Pelagians,* because they have
refused

refused his *Tenet*, concerning the absolute damnation of Infants departing this life, before they were baptized [a].

a Aug. *Epist.* 106. Parvulos non baptizatos, vitam habere non posse, ac per hoc quaˉnlibet tolerabilius omnibus qui etiam propria peccata committunt, tamen æterna morte mulctari. *Id. d. pec. Mer. & Remiss. li.* 1. ca. 16. Et li. 2. ca. 4.

A seventh Passage of Brother B.

All were the true bred Children of the Church of *England*, &c. who maintained *Brother B.* his dictats concerning the old Sabbath, and the Lord's-day; *witnesse, Master Cartwright; Master Fenne; Old Master Gilby; Master Snape; Master Lord; Master Dod,* M*r*. *Cleaver,* M*r*. *Oxenbridge, Master Sheere-wood, Master Iohnson, Master Nutter,* &c.

An eighth Passage of Brother B.

The fourth Commandement is simply and intirely morall, binding Vs Christians to observe the Lord's-Day. *The* reason is, because the Law of the fourth Commandement, according to the proper, and literall sence thereof, was given to the Iewes only, for keeping holy the Saturday, and not to the Gentiles, for the observation of Sunday.

A ninth Passage of Brother B.

The Holy Apostles presently, and immediately, after Christ's Ascension, taught and commanded all Christians to observe the Lord's-Day weekely,

weekely and to renounce the Old Sabbath. *The reason, because Saint Paul some twenty yeares after Christ's Ascension*[a], commanded the Corinthians, to give Almes upon the first day of the weeke, 1 Cor. 16. 2. and Saint *Iohn* many yeares after that stiled Sunday by the name of *the Lord's Day.*

[a] Chytr. *in Cronol.* Anno Christi quinquagessimo quinto, venit Paulus in Troadem, & inde in Macedoniam.

A Tenth Passage of Brother B.

The first day of every weeke throughout the whole yeare, is the Sabbath day of the 4th Commandement, because our Saviour *began to rest from some of his Redemptive actions, upon the latter part of Good-Friday: and* because he rested in his grave the whole *Sabbath day* before his Resurrection, and because hee rested as much upon Munday, Tuesday, and upon other dayes following, *as* he did upon Sunday.

An Eleventh Passage of Brother B.

To give Christian people any liberty, to doe any manner of worke, or to *use any bodily exercise or pastime* upon any part of the Sunday, is to imitate the *Pope* in dispensing against God's morall Law. *Proved,* because brother *B.* is able to produce no Divine or Evangelicall Law, *recorded in holy Scripture,* which prohibiteth all bodily exercise, and sober and honest *recreation upon some part of that day.*

A

A Twelfth Passage of Brother B.

It is unlawfull to use any sober and honest recreation, to wit, such as is neither vicious in quality or circumstance, upon any part of the Lord's day: *because* all profane, ungodly, obscene, and lascivious pastime, is prohibited upon that day, and upon all other dayes throughout the yeare: *as* if one should say, it is not lawfull to eat or drink upon Sunday, *because* surfetting and drunkennesse are unlawfull upon that day, and upon all other dayes.

A Thirteenth Passage of Brother B.

The Bishops of the Church of *England* have not power to instruct the inferiour Clergie in matters of Religion, *because* they have not received miraculous grace, *Ex opere operato: Proved*, because brother B. by his *mother wit*, without ordinary grace, or morall honesty, supposeth himselfe qualified like an Apostle, to correct and instruct all men both simple and learned, in the most profound Questions of Theologie.

A Fourteenth Passage of H. B.

It is a grosse Solecisme in Divinity, to admit an Institution to be Apostolicall, and yet to deny it to be of Divine Authority (and consequently

Law and Gospell reconciled. pag. 52.

to make it temporary and mutable,) Proved, because *Episcopall Authority was of an Apostolicall institution* [c]; neverthelesse, according to *Br. R.* the same is not *Divine*: but the *Prelats* of the Church of *England*, who exercise such Authority, are *Vaines of the Pope*: and the maintainers thereof are guided by a *Papall spirit*, Dialog. pag. 3.

[c] Iren. *lib. 3. ca. 3.* Fundantes igitur & instruentes beati Apostoli Ecclesiam, Lino Episcopatû administrandæ Ecclesiæ tradiderunt. Succedit autem ei Anacletꝰ, post eû, tertio loco ab Apostolis Episcopatû sortitur Clemens. Polycarpus in Asia, in ea quæ est Smyrnis Ecclesia constituto Episcopus (ab Apostolis) Tertul. *c. Hær. cap 32.* Hier. *Catalog. in Clement. Ignatio. Polycarpo, &c.*

A Fifteenth Passage of H. B.

The fourth Commandement being a part of the Law written in *Adam's* heart, needed not any expresse Commandement more than the rest [d]: *Proved*, because it was made knowne by *Divine Revelation* only, and not by a naturall impression, that God created Heaven and Earth in six dayes, and rested the seventh: and if the observation of the Sabbath was commanded *Adam*, the same was the Saturday Sabbath of every weeke, and not the Sunday; and God Almighty himselfe appointed the first day of the Weeke, to be one of the six working dayes.

[d] *Ib. pag. 42.*

A Sixteenth Passage of H. B.

Ib. pag. 45.

The seventh Day being an inseparable Circumstance of the substance of the fourth Commandement, cannot be separated from the Sabbath. *The* Reason, because Christians were taught by *the Apostles*, to make the first day of the week their weekly Festivall, and not the seventh day.

A

(155)

A Seventeenth Passage of H. B.

To rest from all labour, is of the very Essence of the Sabbath: The Reason, because our Saviour maintained, that some labour, which was not of absolute necessity, might lawfully be used upon the Sabbath-day.

Ib. pag. 47.

An Eighteenth Passage of H. B.

Who can deny the keeping of the Sabbath to be morall, but he must withall proclaime open enmity to God's worship and Man's salvation. The reason, because the Apostles taught Christians to observe the Lord's-day, being not the Sabbath of the fourth Commandement, but a new Holy day grounded upon the Resurrection of Christ.

Ib. pag. 41.

A Nineteenth Passage of H. B.

The Commandement of the Sabbath is morall, and so no lesse perpetuall than all the rest: The reason, because it was a shadow of good things to come; and it was abrogated by the Apostles, and changed into another day.

Ib. pag. 38.

X‡ *The*

The last remarkable Observation concerning Br. B.

It is lawfull, when a man cannot otherwise solve an Objection, to passe by both *the Premisses of an Argument*, propounded in due forme, and to deny the *Conclusion, for* example:

No Law which is mutable in respect of the proper materiall Object, is a Law of Nature.

But the fourth Commandement of the Decalogue, was mutable in respect of the proper materiall Object.

Ergo the Law of the fourth Commandement was not a Precept of the Law of Nature.

Againe, no morall action is unlawfull, unlesse it be prohibited by some *Divine Law*, expresse, or virtuall, or by *some humane or Ecclesiasticall Law.*

But bodily exercise or Recreation, not being vicious in quality or circumstance, (if it bee used upon some part of the Holy day) is prohibited by no Divine Law expresse, or virtuall; nor by any humane, or Ecclesiasticall Law.

Ergo, some bodily exercise or Recreation, not being vicious in quality or circumstance, may be permitted and used upon some part of the Holy day.

This *Doctor indocilis*, when hee meeteth with any such Arguments, will not be so simple as to trouble himselfe about the Premisses (as the *Subtle Logitians* use to doe) *but* he holdeth it a more

commodious

commodious, and compendious way, to passe by *the Premisses* with humble silence; and then to spend his fury upon *the conclusion*, raving and declaiming against his *Opposites* in manner following.

1 I note how poorely he playes the *Divine, or Doctor.*

2 The Adversary hath abused the Scripture.

3 It is a *Lunaticke* Opinion.

4 *H. B.* hath shewed it to be *absurd, and ridiculous.*

5 It makes mee *tremble* to thinke, and it amazeth me, how one *White* is contrary to another.

6 This seemes strange to mee, that so *great a Clerk, as Francis White,* should so farre forget himselfe.

7 It will be *a cooling Carde,* and no small disgrace *to his Lordship.*

8 He once approved a book, which *containes and maintaines many and sundry Tenets both Pelagian and Popish :* and one Capitall and enormious error is found in the same (taken out of S. *Iohn's* Canonicall Epistle) *to wit, no murderer hath eternall life abiding in him. He that committeth Adultery, committeth sinne: and he that committeth sin, is of the Devill,* and consequently being formerly just, (according to *Br. B.*) hee remaineth in the state of grace, who during his continuance in sin without actuall Repentance is of the Devill, and hath not eternall life abiding in him.

9 But let me a little excuse *the good Old man, and* the rather because the *Puritans* sticke not to cast him in the teeth with *White died Blacke.*

10 In

10 In the meane time, it is good policy a little *to pull in the Hornes*, and perhaps the Buzze may somewhat possesse *the good Old man* with a Panick feare, lest not only he loose what he hath, but, which is much more, what his many merits may hope for: saving that *Saints merits are* not so high flowne in the Church of *England*, but they are easily over soared *by Simon Magus*, flying to the top of every Pinacle of the highest Temple upon Angels wings.

11. Examine, I pray thee, whether the long custome of *Court-smoothing*, and Eare-pleasing, specially in Divine matters, have not bred such a delicacy in the soules tast, as that *down right Zeale* [a], for God's glory, can hardly finde a stomacke to take it downe, or digest it, but is rejected as a bitter Pill or Potion of such Patients, as account the Remedy worse than the Disease.

12. How many yet are there in these dayes, who would be counted *Bishops of Christ's flocke*, and not Popish, or Antichristian, who yet looke to little else, but the silencing of such as stumble at their *Ceremonies and Hierarchie*.

Now these, and other such like scandalous, and irreverent calumniations are vented by *H. B.* (who stileth *the Puritan a reformed Christian* [b]) Instead of reall answer and solution of such Arguments, as confound his erroneous, and presumptuous dictats.

[a] Jam. 3. 14. *If ye have envie, bitter zeale, envying and strife in your hearts, glory not.*

[b] H. B. *Plea to an Appeale, as he baits to bee reformed, so one peece of his Sermon must be an invective against a Reformed Christian, his Puritan.*

The

The Conclusion.

THE Author of the late Treatise of the Sabbath-day against *Th. Brabourne*, having duly and impartially examined a briefe Answer, digested Dialogue-wise, betweene *A.* and *B.* is able to observe nothing at all therein, materiall, substantiall, or subservient to truth: *but* the whole Dialogue consisteth of vaine jangling, absurd disputing, factious cavelling; and his maine Position, *to wit,* that *the fourth Commandement was naturally morall,* in respect of one particular weekely day, is repugnant to all Orthodoxall Divines, both ancient and moderne, *and* it crosseth his owne Tenet, concerning the observation of the Lord's-Day.

If the man were of a meeke and humble spirit, or a lover of truth, *we* might perswade him to entertaine a fairer meanes of resolution, than *his irregular and unlicensed Dialogue way: To* wit, if hee finde himselfe unsatisfied touching the question of the Sabbath: he should addresse himselfe to some learned and judicious Persons [a], and submit himselfe to a private conference, as *Theoph. Brabourne* did: *for* there is no meanes so profitable, so speedie, and ready for discovery of truth as this.

[a] Bernard Ep. 82, Plerisq; imo cunctis sapientibus contingere solet, in rebus videlicet dubiis, plus alieno se quam proprio judicio credere.

In

In writing and printing *unlicensed Pamphlets* [a], there useth to bee much mistaking, sometimes of the true state of the question, and many times of the Adversaries Tenet, likewise false and sophisticall Argumentation, mis-understanding of termes, impertinent digressions, tautologies, and unnecessary repetitions, false citing of Authors, &c. *But* in conference the former things may easily be avoyded, or presently be discovered.

Now if the *Author of the Dialogue* (or if any other, that is unsatisfied) think good to entertaine the former course, he may reape much benefit by it, and thereby declare himselfe to be a lover of Vnitie, Verity, and Peace.

But on the contrary, the venting of *Lawlesse, and contentious Pamphlets*, is infamous, scandalous, and factious: it fomenteth schisme, and contention in Church, and State; it disquieteth and offendeth peaceable and godly mindes; the same provoketh publike authority: and the Adversaries of our Doctrine and Religion, are thereby much confirmed in their error.

Therefore I desire all those, who are lovers of truth and sincerity, to be men of peace [b], and to shew themselves adversaries to schisme [c], and contention in the Church and State, wherein they enjoy *their lively-hood and their liberty*.

And for your selfe, *Dialogue B*. cease to affect popular applause; *be* not overwise and wilfull in your owne conceits; *referre* the handling, and deciding of profound Questions of Theologie, to such persons as are qualified with judgement and

learning;

---

[a] H. B. *Plea to an Appeale, Truth she complaines of hard usage, how shee is driven to seeke corners, sith shee cannot passe the presse, cum privilegio.*

[b] *Cypr. de simpl. Prœl.* Pacem quærere debet & sequi filius pacis, à dissensionis malo continere linguam suam debet, qui novit & diligit vinculum Charitatis.

[c] *Id. de unit. Eccles.* Possidere non potest indumentum Christi, qui scindit & dividit Ecclesiã Christi.

learning, and with greater humility and modesty than your selfe [a]: *Nec erubescas de commutatione sententia tua; Non es enim tantæ authoritatis & fama, ut errasse te pudeat:* Thinke it no disgrace to alter your opinion; for you are not of so great Authority or fame, as that it can be any shame for you, to relinquish your error.

Also consider impartially with what irreverent language [b] you have entreated many worthy Fathers and Pillars of our Church; and with what bitter and envious zeale you have traduced *conformable* Persons of very good quality: and what scandall you have given to many people, by abating (as much in you lyeth) their love, and due respect towards that Religion, and forme of Church-government, which is setled in our State.

Lastly, consider well Saint *Hierom* his Instruction: *Bonum est obedire Majoribus, parere Præfectis* [c], *& post regulam Scripturarum, vitæ suæ rationem ab aliis discere, Nec Præceptore uti pessimo, præsumptione sua.* "It is a good and safe way for people of "meaner quality to be teachable, and obedient to their "superiours; to be guided and instructed by such as "are of greater perfection than themselves: and after "the rule of holy Scripture, to order the course of their "actions by direction of others, but in no wise to make "presumption, which is a perverse Counsellor, to be "their Leader.

Salomon's Counsell is: *Heare instruction, and bee wise, and refuse it not,* Pro. 9. 33. *Hee that loveth instruction, loveth knowledge: but he that hateth Correction is a foole,* Pro. 12. *When Pride commeth, then commeth shame, but with the lowly is wisdome,*

a Hier. *c. Ruffin.* Navem agere ignarus navis timet: Abrotonum ægro non audet propinare, nisi qui didicit, dare: Quod medicorum est promittunt medici, tractant fabrilia fabri.

b Cypr. *de unit. Ecclesiæ* Lingua Christum confessa non sit maledica; non turbulenta, non convictis & litibus perstrepens audiatur: non contra fratres & Dei sacerdotes, serpentis venena jaculatur.

c *Erasm.* Schol. in Hieron. *In some Copies it is read* Præfectis, *and in some other* Perfectis.

Y

dome, Pro. 11. *Only by pride doth man make contention, but with the well-advised is wisedome*, Pro. 13.

Now let all this which hath beene spoken perswade *Dialogue B.* to cast away from him, pride, envy, and contention; to cease to be *arrogant* [d], to learne yet at the last, to understand his distance [e], and in the feare of *God* to humble and submit himselfe to his learned, lawfull, and godly superiors: *And* let him not give just occasion to have *Salomon's* sentence applyed unto him, *Though thou shouldest bray a foole in a morter, like wheate with a Pestle, yet will not his folly depart from him*, Prov. 27. ver. 22.

[d] Chrys. *in Rom. hom.* 20. Nihil hominem adeo stultum facit quemadmodum Arrogantia.

[e] *Ib.* Qui seipsum ignorat, quomodo quæ supra se sunt cognoscat? Quemadmodú enim qui phrenesi laborat, cum seipsum non ignoscat, & oculus cum ipse cæcus sit omnia reliqua membra in tenebris sunt: ita & Arrogantia se habet.

FINIS.